The Catholic Church

The Catholic Church:

Easy Answers to Frequently Asked Questions

Joseph Domfeh-Boateng, JCL. PhD

Copyright © 2014 by Joseph Domfeh-Boateng, JCL. PhD.
Foreword by Rev. Thomas Oppong-Febiri, JCD

Library of Congress Control Number:		2014903050
ISBN:	Hardcover	978-1-4931-7436-2
	Softcover	978-1-4931-7437-9
	eBook	978-1-4931-7435-5

This book was printed in the United States of America.

Scriptures taken from *Christian Community Bible: Catholic Pastoral Edition*
Sixth Edition Copyright @ Bernard Hurault also from *GOOD NEWS BIBLE WITH DEUTERCANONICALS/APOCRYPHA* TODAY'S ENGLISH VERSION
ABS AMERICAN BIBLE SOCIETY, NEW YORK 104891-104892.

Rev. date: 03/04/2014

To order additional copies of this book, contact:
Xlibris LLC
1-888-795-4274
www.Xlibris.com
Orders@Xlibris.com
543901

CONTENTS

Dedication

This book is dedicated to my parents: Peter Kwame Domfeh and Agatha Kissiwaa Domfeh, whose caring love cultivated and nurtured the Catholic faith in my family.

Nihil obstat: Rev. Msgr. George Kwame Kumi, PhD
                   The Vicar General, Catholic Diocese of Sunyani, Ghana
                   Date: November 1, 2013

Imprimatur: Most Rev. Matthew Kwasi Gyamfi, DD, PhD
                 Catholic Bishop of Sunyain, Ghana
                 November 8, 2013

FOREWORD

A story is told of an aged staunch Catholic who was asked by his friends to define the Catholic Church that he was so fond of. Without any theological formation, but on the basis of his personal experience, he defined the Catholic Church as a vast or oceanic institution that embodies all that is best and worst in human beings. Indeed, the Catholic Church is like an ocean. The Catholic Church is divine and human; old and young attached great importance to tradition, yet were attentive to new trends. The Church adores and worships the one and only God; yet she honors and venerates the heroes and heroines of her faith, and her members are made up of saints and sinners, pilgrims and the triumphant, the poor and the prosperous, doubters and believers. The Church, in the words of Karl Adam, is a "union of contraries. But contraries are not contradictions." In the more than two thousand years of her existence, there has always been a union between her interior and exterior strengths, her material and spiritual wealth, her prosperity and poverty, her terrestrial and celestial concerns, her exhortation of marriage and her treasure of celibacy.

This book, *The Catholic Church: Easy Answers to Frequently Asked Questions,* explores this oceanic institution and attempts to explain the beauty of the contraries in the Catholic Church. The author guides his readers through the operational structures of the Church by answering questions people ask on the legalistic and pneumatic dimensions of the Church, its hierarchical structure, the basic equality of its members as pilgrims, its sacramental life, its beliefs and practices, and its cherished sacramentals. The author is modest and acknowledges that his book is just a drop in the ocean in terms of describing what the Catholic Church is or what it does.

This book is highly recommended for seminarians, for it enables them to answer questions often posed to them. It is also a vital tool for pastors in sharing the Catholic faith with the flock they minister to. It is good material for seminary professors, helping them to refresh and to update themselves. This book is also a good source of information for Catholics who desire to deepen their understanding of the Church and for non-Catholics who seek to know more about the Catholic Church. In a strict sense, the book is not a catechetical instruction book, since it is more informative than formative.

This book had a modest beginning as a private conversation of a pastoral disposition with an enquiring mind about the Catholic Church. The author designed the entire book in a question-and-answer pattern which is easy to read. It is not designed to be read from cover to cover; readers may choose to look for answers to specific questions that are of interest to them.

I believe that this book will help readers to know and understand the ancient and vast institution known as the Catholic Church. It is my prayer that the book will attain its ultimate goal by helping readers not only to be fascinated with the Catholic Church as a divine and human institution, but to have a personal experience with God the Father who has redeemed the human race through Jesus Christ, who founded the Church, and the Holy Spirit, who is continually present in the Church.

Rev. Thomas Oppong-Febiri, JCD
December 8, 2013

ACKNOWLEDGMENTS

I must admit that this book has received insightful suggestions and encouragement from various scholars. It has, thus, benefited from the work of many different hands and minds. It will, therefore, be a difficult task for me to mention all the individuals who have helped at different stages in shaping the ideas in this book. However, some special individuals must be acknowledged for their extraordinary assistance.

I am particularly indebted to His Eminence Edward Cardinal Egan, the Archbishop Emeritus of New York, for reading the manuscript page by page and giving insightful comments and suggestions. I thank His Eminence Cardinal Egan for the generous assistance and systematic guidance he has given me in writing the book.

Special thanks go to Rev. Thomas Oppong-Febiri for taking time out of his busy parish ministry to read through the manuscript, giving various suggestions and writing the foreword to the book. I thank Rev. Oppong-Febiri for his help. I am also grateful to various scholars whose books I consulted at different stages, gathering materials for this book.

Last but not least, I am most grateful to many friends, both ordained and non-ordained, for their friendship, support, and care. This book would not have been possible without their friendship and encouragement.

I am grateful to all of you for the help you have given me at different stages when writing this book; for your insightful comments and constructive suggestions helped to shape the ideas in the book, though I take sole ownership of its content.

THE AUTHOR

Joseph Domfeh-Boateng is a priest of the Catholic Diocese of Sunyani, Ghana. He holds a PhD in Educational Administration and Supervision from Fordham University, New York and a Licentiate in Canon Law from St. Paul University, Ottawa, Canada. He is the founder and executive director of the Giving to Ghana Foundation, Inc. and currently serves as a parochial vicar at St. Patrick's Church, Bedford, New York.

GENERAL INTRODUCTION

One lovely summer afternoon, I had a phone call from a friend of mine. He wanted to know the difference between Catholicism and Christianity. In other words, he wanted to know whether Catholics are Christians or not. His question triggered a long and exciting discussion about what it means to be a Catholic. This friend was very appreciative that our phone conversation and subsequent discussion on the subject matter enabled him to have a better understanding and appreciation of the Church he loves. In this book, the term "Church" refers to the Catholic Church.

Our conversation on that lovely afternoon and the appreciation this friend showed for my systematic guidance sparked the idea for the writing of this book. Like this friend of mine, many people have specific questions about the operational structures of the Church and are looking for direct answers, ones not easily found in Sunday homilies or in a parish Bible study group. This book attempts to answer some basic questions people frequently ask about the Catholic Church. Thus, the primary purpose of this book is to take its reader through the operational structures of the Catholic Church and its basic beliefs and practices regarding the Church's governance, leading the reader to a better understanding and appreciation of the Catholic Church. The book is not designed to be read from cover to cover; readers can look for answers to their specific questions.

This book, thus, serves as a tool for those who are interested in understanding how the Catholic Church is governed and what informs and directs its activities. The book particularly serves as a tool for those who minister in the Church, such as priests, sisters, deacons, lay associates, and catechists. Young men in the seminaries preparing for the priesthood will also find the book useful during their formative years. Plus, this book is useful for anyone who is interested in knowing more about the Catholic Church.

Overview of the Book

The book is divided into six chapters. Chapter 1 explores what constitutes the Catholic Church. In the first chapter, I attempt to answer questions such as these: What is the Catholic Church? What constitutes the Catholic Church? Are members of the Catholic Church Christians? How does one become a member of the Catholic Church? And finally, what is the difference between the Church of Christ and the Catholic Church?

The second chapter answers questions on the operational structures of the Catholic Church. Specific questions addressed in the chapter include the basic operational structures of the Church, the people who exercise the supreme authority in the Church, the members of the College of Bishops, the limits of ecclesiastical authority, the governance of the Diocese of Rome, the governance of the universal Church, the Roman Curia, papal legates, and the consultative organs of the Roman Pontiff. In the third chapter, I discuss questions on the organizational structure of particular Churches, the selection and appointment of a diocesan bishop, the pastoral governance of a diocesan church, the diocesan curia, the consultative organs of a diocesan bishop, the governance of a diocese when the diocesan see is impeded or vacant, and supra-diocesan church groupings. In chapter 4, I examine specific questions about the parish church, its relationship with the diocesan bishop, its governance, the principal functions of a parish priest, the primary functions of a parish church, and its relationship with other parish churches in a given diocese and the universal Church. Chapter 5 addresses questions on the teaching authority of the Church and on her sanctifying and healing offices. In chapter 6, I discuss questions of Catholic beliefs and practices. In this chapter, I try to answer questions on the sacramentals, their relevance to the life of a Catholic believer, the liturgy of hours, the relevance of ecclesiastical funerals, and the veneration of saints, relics, and sacred images. This chapter further explores questions on the differences between a church and other places of worship, like chapels, shrines, and basilicas. It also examines holy days of obligation, ecumenical councils, and the church's relationship with non-Catholic Christian Churches and ecclesial communities.

ABBREVIATIONS

AA   *Vatican* II, decretum *Apostolicam Actuositatem:* The Decree on the Apostolate of the Laity, November 18, 1965.

c.   canon.

cc.   canons.

CCC   Catechism of the Catholic Church (1994), Vatican City.

CCE   Congregation for Catholic Education.

CD   *Vatican* II, decretum *Christus Dominus:* The decree on the Pastoral Office of Bishops, October 28, 1965.

DE   *Directory for the Application of Principles and Norms on Ecumenism;* Vatican City, 1998.

DPM   *Divinus Prefectionis Magister* (Pope John Paul II, Apostolic Constitution, January 25, 1983).

DV   *Vatican* II, decretum *Dei Verbum:* The Dogmatic Constitution on Divine Revelation, November 18, 1965.

ECE   *Ex Corde Ecclesiae:* Apostolic Constitution on Catholic Universities, August 1990.

LG   *Vatican* II, decretum *Lumen Gentium:* The dogmatic Constitution on the Church, November 21, 1964.

NCCB   National Conference of Catholic Bishops (USA)

OE   *Orientalium Ecclesiarum:* The Decree on the
                Catholic Oriental Church

PB   *Pastor Bonus:* Apostolic Constitution on *the Good
                Shepherd,* November 1988.

UDG   *Universi Dominici Gregis:* Apostolic Constitution on
                norms on the funeral of a Supreme Pontiff and
                election of a new Supreme Pontiff, February 22,
                1996.

UR   Vatican II decretum *Unitatis Redintegratio:* The
                decree on Ecumenism, November 21, 1964.

CHAPTER 1

The Catholic Church

What is the Catholic Church? Are its members Christians?

These questions will be approached from three directions.
1. What is the Catholic Church?
2. Who is a Christian?
3. What do Catholics believe?
After exploring these questions, one can draw conclusions about whether Catholics are Christians or not.

What is the Catholic Church?

The word "Catholic" is derived from combining two Greek words: *kata,* which means "every," "including all," and *holos,* which is the root of the word "whole" or "general" and refers to different elements uniting and working together. The two words combine to form *katholos,* which is translated to mean "including everybody, all people are welcome, forming a community of believers that reflects diversity and unity in faith." The word "Catholic" in this sense means everybody. Ignatius, the bishop of Antioch (d. 107) was the first to use the term "Catholic" to describe the early Christian community, when he said, "Where Jesus is, there is the Catholic Church." Ignatius of Antioch used this expression to mean the whole Church, as distinct from the parochial and local churches.

The Catholic Church is a worldwide Christian religion united together as one community of faith through its bishops under the headship of the Bishop of Rome, the pope. The Catholic Church is distinguished from all other Christian Churches and Protestant ecclesial communities by three elements: the profession of faith, the sacraments, and ecclesiastical governance (c. 205). Donovan (1997) described the Catholic Church as "a living community of faith, a community with its own distinctive rituals and structures, its own patterns of individual and collective religious life" (p. 1). As a faith community, the Catholic Church has gone through a very long and complex history of over two thousand years. In the course of its long, winding history, the Catholic Church has encountered many different cultures and some very confusing historical situations, which together have helped shape its distinctive identity, culture, and discipline (Donovan, 1997).

Who is a Christian?

The word "Christian," according to its Greek etymology, means one who believes in Jesus Christ as Lord and Savior and belongs to the people of Christ. The early disciples of Christ Jesus were first called Christians (in Greek, *Christianoi, "Christ's people")* in Antioch (Acts 11:25). Antioch, Rome, and Alexandria were the three most important cities in the Roman Empire. Antioch was located at the junction of the land routes between Asia Minor, Mesopotamia, and Egypt. Some of the early believers who fled Jerusalem after the martyrdom of St. Stephen came to Antioch, where they focused their preaching on the Gentiles. It was in Antioch that they founded the first mixed community of faith, made up of both Jews and Gentiles. The Christian message hinges on the belief that Jesus of Nazareth, who is the Son of God, was condemned, crucified on the Cross, died, and rose again on the third day, and has become the source of salvation for all who believe in him as Lord and Savior. Whoever accepts his message as recorded in the Holy Scripture and confesses him as Lord and Savior belongs to *Christianoi, Christ's people.*

What do Catholics believe?

Like all Christians, the members of the Catholic Church are monotheists. They believe in one God, who is the Creator, Sustainer, Ruler, Judge of the universe and the Father of all people. They believe that God reveals himself at different stages of human salvation as God the Father, God the Son, and God the Holy Spirit. They also believe that Jesus Christ, God the Son, is of the same substance with God the Father, and that both deserve the same worship, adoration, and majesty. Catholics believe that God the Holy Spirit proceeds from the Father and the Son. Thus, the belief in the Triune God, the three persons in the Godhead, is a central doctrine in the Catholic Church, for everything Catholics do begins and ends with this Trinitarian formula. Catholics believe that Jesus Christ is the visible image of the invisible God. They also believe that prior to the coming of Jesus Christ, God offered a covenant to man that prophets such as Moses, Elijah, Elisha, Isaiah, Jeremiah, Ezekiel, and John the Baptist taught man to hope for salvation and that in the fullness of time, God sent his Son as the Savior of the world. Catholics believe that Jesus Christ, who is the Son of God, was condemned to death, was crucified on the Cross, and died, that God raised him up on the third day, and that he has become the source of salvation for all who believe in him. Catholics accept his message as recorded in the Holy Scripture and confess him as Lord and Savior, and therefore, they belong to Christ's people and are Christians. Catholics believe and accept both the Old and New Testaments as the Word of God. Like all Christians, Catholics believe that Jesus Christ will come again to judge the living and the dead, the righteous will be sent to heaven, and the condemned will be sent to hell.

In addition to beliefs that are common to all Christians, Catholics acknowledge the Blessed Virgin Mary as the mother of Jesus Christ and the mother of the Church. They also believe in the existence of saints and angels, who constantly intercede for the pilgrim Church. They believe that their Church was founded by Jesus Christ himself and has given it all it needs for the salvation of souls. Another central doctrine in the Catholic Church is the belief in the Real Presence of Jesus Christ in the Holy Eucharist; that is, Jesus Christ is really and truly present, body and soul in the Eucharist. Thus, whoever receives the Holy Eucharist, Catholics believe, receives Jesus Christ himself, the body, blood, soul, and divinity. The basis of this doctrine is found in Jesus's promise to remain with the Church until the end of time (Mt 28:20). On the basis of the above, one can conclude that Catholics are Christians because they believe and accept the Gospel of Jesus Christ.

The Catholic Church is the largest Christian denomination in the world. The members of the Catholic Church are united together through their bishops under the leadership of the Roman Pontiff, the pope. Though Catholics are Christians, they are different from other Christians, because the Catholic Church has its own distinctive rituals, traditions, culture, discipline, and governing structures. The Bishop of Rome is the spiritual leader of the Catholic Church.

How many autonomous Churches constitute the Catholic Church?

The Catholic Church consists of twenty-two autonomous (*sui iuris*) Churches; each with its own hierarchy, traditions, and discipline. All these autonomous Churches, though juridically distinct, are united under the leadership and pastoral ministry of the pope, the Bishop of Rome. The chart below spells out the various autonomous churches that constitute the Holy Catholic Church.

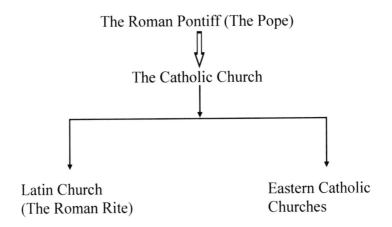

The twenty-one Eastern Churches are as follows:
1. *Alexandrian Rite* (Coptic and Ethiopian Church)
2. *Antiochere Rite* (Malankar Church, Maronite Church, and Syrian Church)
3. *Byzantine Rite* (Albanian Church, Byelorussian Church, Bulgarian Church, Greek Church, Italo-Albanian Church, Yugoslavian Church, Melkite Church,

Romanian Church, Russian Church, Ruthenian Church, Slovakian Church, Ukrainian Church and the Hungarian Church).
4. *Chaldean Rite* (Chaldean and Malabar Churches)
5. *Armenian Rite* (Armenian Church).

As shown in the chart above, the Catholic Church "is made up of the faithful who are organically united in the Holy Spirit by the same faith, sacraments, and the same government" (*OE,* 1). However, the faithful of the Catholic Church fall under different groups under their own hierarchy and thus form various particular Churches or rites. Although the members of the Catholic Church differ somewhat among themselves in liturgy, ecclesiastical discipline, and spiritual traditions, they are "all equally entrusted to the pastoral guidance of the Roman Pontiff, who by God's appointment is successor to Blessed Peter in primacy over the universal Church" (*OE,* 3). The Latin and Eastern Catholic churches are "of equal rank, so that none of them is superior to the others because of its rite" (*OE, 3*). They have the same rights and obligations regarding the proclamation of the Gospel of Jesus Christ to the whole world as commanded by Christ himself (Mk 16:15; Mt 28:19-20). The Catholic Church carries this obligation under the leadership and direction of the Roman Pontiff.

Does the Catholic Church have only one Code of Canon Law?

No, the Catholic Church has two different Codes of Canon Laws. The *1983 Code of Canon Law* regulates the internal organizational structure and the behavioral life of the members of the Latin Church while the *Code of Canons of the Eastern Churches,* promulgated by Pope John Paul II on October 18, 1990, regulates the structures and life of the Eastern Catholic Churches.

Is there any difference between the Christ's Church and the Catholic Church?

Yes, the Second Vatican Council speaks of the difference between Christ's Church and the Catholic Church in the *LG*, 8. The conciliar fathers declared that Christ's Church, which, in the Nicene Creed we profess to be one, holy, catholic, and apostolic, subsists in the Catholic Church. The Catholic Church is governed by Peter's successor and the bishops in communion with him (*LG*, 8; Flannery, 1998, p. 357). The Second Vatican Council further declared that many elements of our salvation, sanctification, and truth are found outside the visible confines of the Catholic Church (*LG*, 8). It is with this new understanding that the Second Vatican Council exhorted Catholic Christians to treat members of other churches and ecclesial communities, who are also members of the Church of Christ, with respect and dignity.

How does one become a member of the Church of Christ?

One becomes a member of Christ's Church through baptism. It is by one's baptism that "one is incorporated into the Christ's Church and is constituted a person in it with the duties and rights which are proper to Christians in keeping with their conditions, insofar as they are in ecclesiastical communion and unless a legitimately issued sanction stands in the way" (c. 96). The members of Christ's Church, according to Huels (2009), include baptized Catholics and baptized non-Catholic Christians. Thus, in addition to Catholic Christians, the baptized members of Orthodox Churches, that is, the members of all Eastern non-Catholic churches, are also members of Christ's Church. The following ecclesial communities: African Methodist Episcopal, Amish, Anglican, Assembly of God, Baptist, Evangelical United Brethren, Church of Brethren, Church of God, Congregational Churches, Disciples of Christ, Episcopalians, Evangelical Churches, Lutherans, Methodists, the Liberal Catholic Church, Old Catholics, Old Roman Catholics, the Church of the Nazarene, the Polish National Church, the Presbyterian Church, Reformed Church, and the United Church of Christ all have a valid baptism, and their members are incorporated into the Church of Christ.

How does one become a member of the Catholic Church?

Membership in the Catholic Church is gained through a valid baptism or reception into full communion of one who was validly baptized outside the Catholic Church. The membership of the Catholic Church consists of those baptized Catholics who are in full communion with the Catholic Church and are united with Christ in his mystical body by bonds of the profession of faith, the sacraments, and ecclesiastical governance. As noted above, not all of the members of Christ's Church are in full communion with the Catholic Church. The Catholic Christians are different from all other followers of Christ Jesus because they are united with the visible structure of the Church by the bonds of the Catholic faith and the sacraments and by ecclesiastical governance under the authority of the Bishop of Rome and the bishops in communion with him. Although the members of the separated Eastern Churches and Protestant ecclesial communities are Christians, they are not members of the Catholic Church because of some differences in doctrine and ecclesiastical governance.

What is a valid baptism? How does one's baptism become valid?

For a person's baptism to be valid and thus incorporate him or her into the mystery of the Church, it must have the proper *matter* and *form.*
Matter: For validity, the baptism must be celebrated with true water, either by pouring, sprinkling, or immersion (c. 849).
Form: The proper form of baptism is the Trinitarian formula. Basically, the minister must say, for instance, "John, I baptize you in the name of the Father, and of the Son, and of the Holy Spirit."

Are there any conditions that a non-baptized person needs to fulfill before he or she is baptized in the church?

Before one receives baptism in the Church, one must repent of one's sins (Acts 2:38), profess a personal faith in the Lord Jesus, and accept his Gospel. On the celebration of a valid sacrament of baptism, the *1983 Code of Canon Law* declares, "Baptism, the gateway to the sacraments and necessary for salvation by actual reception, or at least by desire, is validly conferred only by a washing of true water with the proper form of words. Through baptism, men and women are freed from sin, are reborn as children of God, and configured to Christ by an indelible character, are incorporated into the church" (c. 849).

What is the baptism of desire?

There are those people "who, through no fault of their own, do not know the Gospel of Christ, or his Church, but who nevertheless seek God with a sincere heart, and, moved by grace, try in their actions to do his Will as they know it through the dictates of their conscience— those too may achieve eternal salvation. Nor shall divine providence deny the assistance necessary for salvation to those who, without any fault of their own, have not yet arrived at an explicit knowledge of God, and who, not without grace, strive to lead a good life" (*LG*, 16; Flannery, 1998, pp. 1034-1035). There is another type of baptism, the baptism of blood; that may also lead to salvation. Though both baptism of desire and baptism of blood may lead to salvation, only the actual reception of baptism produces theological effects. The theological effects of baptism include:

- It frees us from sin, original and personal sins;
- It configures us to the personhood of Christ, thereby incorporating us into the mystery of his death and resurrection (Rom 6:4);
- It imprints an indelible mark on our souls; and
- It incorporates us into the Church with rights and obligations.

Why does the Catholic Church administer infant baptism?

A brief exploration into the background of why the Catholic Church baptizes infants will lead to a better understanding and appreciation. In the Old Testament, the Lord God entered into a covenant with Abraham. In describing the terms of that covenant, the Lord God says:

> Every male among you shall be circumcised. You shall circumcise your foreskin and that will be the sign of the covenant between me and you. When he is eight days old, every male among you will be circumcised, generation

after generation; those born in your household or bought from a foreigner as slaves. Whether born in your household or bought to be slaves, they must be circumcised. So my covenant will be written in your flesh as an everlasting covenant. Any uncircumcised male, who has not been circumcised in the flesh, will be cut off from his people for having broken my covenant. (Gn 17:10-14)

In the above biblical passage, the Lord God clearly sets out the conditions by which one becomes a member of the chosen people. It is through the ritual of circumcision that male-born children are incorporated into the family of God under the headship of Abraham.

In his earthly ministry, Jesus established a new people of God, who are often referred to as the new Israel, and its membership is open to Jews and Gentiles alike through the sacrament of baptism. Before his ascension, Jesus commissioned his disciples to go into the whole world and to make disciples of all nations, baptizing them in the name of the Father, and of the Son, and of the Holy Spirit (Mk 16:15-16; Mt 28:18-20). These were among the last words of Jesus before he ascended to his Father.

Does this practice of baptizing infants have any biblical foundation?

Right from its inception, the Church has been administering the sacrament of baptism not only to adults, but to infants and children as well. In his first powerful and inspired preaching, after the Pentecost experience in Acts 2:1-13, Peter invites his audience to repent and to be baptized, so that they may be saved. He concludes his teaching with these words: "For the promise of God was made to you and your children" (Acts 2:39). Children are, therefore, invited to receive salvation, and since baptism is the necessary means of receiving salvation, children cannot and should not be denied the sacrament of baptism.

Lydia, a God-fearing woman from Thyatira City, was baptized together with her household (Acts 16:15); and Paul and Silas baptized the former guard of their jail and his whole household (Acts 16:35). A leading man from Crispus, along with his whole household, became believers and were baptized (Acts 18:8); Cornelius and his household became God-fearing and received baptism (Acts 10:2); and Paul baptized Stephana's family (1 Cor 1:16). Though one cannot conclude with certainty that infants and children were baptized in the synopsis of the biblical passages above, the term "household" presupposes that children or infants were included in the reception of the sacrament of baptism. Moreover, one cannot fathom how Lydia, Cornelius, and the prison guard could possibly exclude their children from receiving salvation, which is made possible through baptism after accepting Jesus Christ as their Lord and Savior.

It is on the basis of the aforementioned understanding and context that the Catholic Church administers the sacrament of baptism to infants and children even though they lack the capacity to make a personal profession of faith in the Lord Jesus. Another traditional reason for this practice is that baptism washes away original sin. Infants or children are baptized on the condition that their parents will bring them up in the practice of the faith. As primary educators in the faith of their children, the *1983 Code of Canon Law* states that parents and godparents of children to be baptized are to receive suitable preparation before their children are baptized (c. 774 § 2; c. 793 § 1). The law does not require parents to give a saint's name to their child at baptism. However, the law requires that "parents, sponsors, and pastors are to take care that a name foreign to Christian sensibilities is not given" (c. 855).

How do children enroll in the various Catholic Churches (*Church sui iuris*)?

Canon 111 § 1 spells out clear rules that are to be applied in determining the proper Church for children under fourteen years of age. The rules state that:

1. If both parents belong to the Latin Church, at the baptism, the child under fourteen years of age is enrolled in the Latin Church;
2. If the father is a Latin Catholic and the mother is an Eastern Catholic, the child may be baptized in either Church. However, if the mother is a Latin Catholic and the father is an Eastern Catholic, the child is to be baptized in the church of his or her

father, that is, Eastern Catholic Church, unless both parents agree to raise the child in the Latin Church. In the absence of such an agreement, or even if the parents did not know this law and raised their child in the Latin Church, the child, in law, belongs to the Eastern Church of his or her father (c. 111 § 1); and

3. A child born of an unwed mother is be baptized in the Church of his or her mother; and a child of unknown parents is to be baptized and enrolled in the ritual Church of his or her guardian.

4. However, a person over fourteen years of age is free to decide his or her own ritual Church.

5. One also needs permission from the Apostolic See to be bi-ritual, that is, to be Eastern Catholic and Latin Catholic at the same time.

The members of the Church are often referred to as the People of God. The membership is grouped into two main categories: clergy and laity (c. 207). The former are those members who have been admitted into holy orders through the reception of the diaconate, while the latter are the remaining members of the people of God. Therefore, we often refer to the people of God as clergy or laity. A third group are members of religious orders and societies of apostolic life. Technically, members of religious communities and societies of apostolic life are either clergy or laity. Members of these orders and societies who have been ordained into the order of the diaconate or presbytery belong to the clergy, and the non-ordained members are lay members of the Church.

Catechumens are "those who ask by explicit choice under the influence of the Holy Spirit to be incorporated into the Church" (c. 206, While they are not yet members, the Church generously responds to their desire to join the Church by guiding them systematically along "the path toward baptism, teaching them Christian doctrine and Christian life, and granting them" (Martin de Agar, 1999, p. 47) rights and "various prerogatives which are proper to Christians").

Who are the clergy? How does one become a cleric?

The clergy are the members of the Church who have been ordained to exercise certain functions in the Church. A male member of the

Catholic Church becomes a cleric through a diaconate ordination and is incardinated in the particular church he is ordained to serve. Through the reception of diaconate ordination, a perpetually professed religious or a definitively incorporated member of a clerical society of apostolic life is incardinated as a cleric in the same institute or society unless, in the case of societies, the constitutions of their order of congregation establish otherwise (c. 266 § 2). For a cleric who has already been incardinated to be validly incardinated in another church, he must obtain a letter of excardination from his original bishop and a letter of incardination from a bishop of the particular church where he wishes to be incardinated. A cleric who has lawfully moved from his own particular church to another local church is, by virtue of the law itself, incardinated in that latter church after five years of ministering in the latter church, if he has declared his intention to be incardinated in writing to both the diocesan bishop of the host diocese and his own diocesan bishop and neither of them raises any objection in writing within four months of receiving the cleric's written request.

The members of the clergy exercise their functions on three different levels: the order of episcopate (bishops), the order of presbytery (priests), and the order of diaconate (deacons). The *Catechism of the Catholic Church* (1994) teaches that priests and bishops are ordained to participate in the ministerial priesthood of Jesus (*CCC,* 1554).

Describing the order of bishops, the Second Vatican Council declared that among those various ministries exercised in the Church from its earliest beginning, the chief place was held by a bishop. The pastoral care of the people of God in a given diocese is entrusted to the pastoral ministry of a diocesan bishop. As shepherds of their flocks, they guide their people as authentic teachers of doctrine, ministers of sacred worship, and ministers in their respective dioceses.

Since those holding the office of bishop are charged with the mission of teaching, preaching, and governing the people of God on their paths to salvation, the fullness of the holy orders is conferred on the bishops through episcopal ordination (*LG,* 21). The Second Vatican Council declared that "episcopal ordination confers, together with the office of sanctifying, the duty also of teaching and ruling" (*LG,* 21). However, the authority to teach, sanctify, and govern that is conferred through episcopal ordination can only be lawfully and validly exercised when the bishops are in hierarchical communion with the Bishop of Rome and other members of the College of Bishops.

Priests are ordained to participate in the priesthood of Jesus Christ under the authority of their bishops or religious superiors. Priests do not participate in the priesthood of their bishops or superiors, but in that of Christ Jesus. The Second Vatican Council points out that through the sacrament of Holy Orders and the anointing of the Holy Spirit, priests:

> are signed with a special character and so are configured to Christ, the priest, in such a way that they are able to act in the person of Christ, the head. Since they share in the function of the apostles in their own degree, priests are given the grace of God to be the ministers of Jesus Christ among nations, fulfilling the sacred task of the Gospel, that the oblation of the Gentiles may be made acceptable to and sanctified in the Holy Spirit. (*PO*, No. 2)

Unlike bishops and priests, deacons are ordained to a ministry of service in the Church and to a community (Acts 6:1-6). Cardinal Kasper (2003) declared that a deacon "is not a 'mini-priest' who fills gaps left where no priests are available, nor is his ministry a mere transitional stage on the path to the priesthood. It is an autonomous ministry; a specific articulation of the ministerial service entrusted to the Church by Jesus Christ" (p. 20). As a minister of service, the deacon is charged in a special way with the Christian service and is "more closely bound to the altar and share in the ministry of preaching" (Cardinal Kasper, 2003, p. 21). Thus, the main functions of deacons include: proclaiming and preaching the Gospel of Jesus Christ and undertaking works of charity for the people of God. The *Catechism of the Catholic Church* (1994) describes the order of diaconate when it says: "deacons are ministers ordained for tasks of service of the church; they do not receive the ministerial priesthood, but (their) ordination confers on them important functions in the ministry of Word, divine worship, and pastoral governance, and the service of charity, tasks which they must carry out under the pastoral authority of their bishops" (CCC. 1570).

People are ordained into the order of episcopate, presbytery, and diaconate for the service of the faith community. Thus, the pope, bishops, priests, and deacons are not ordained for themselves, but rather ordained to fulfill certain critical "tasks and responsibilities related to building up the Church, maintaining its unity, the deepening of its common life" (Donovan, 1997, p. 114). The leadership style of those admitted into holy orders is to be modeled after that of Jesus Christ, who came not to be served, but to serve and to give his life to redeem many (Mt 20:28).

Do the members of the clergy have any specific obligations and rights in the Church?

The members of the clergy have some specific rights and obligations, which can be categorized into strong obligations, prohibited acts and activities, exhortations, and recommendations.

Members of the clergy are obliged to have a special reverence, obedience, and duty to the pope and to their own ordinaries. This obedience demands that they accept and faithfully execute the ecclesiastical offices entrusted to them by their ordinary or superior, unless they are excused by a legitimate impediment or lawfully prohibited to hold ecclesiastical office (c. 274 § 2). Clerics are obliged to pursue the holiness of life, since they have been consecrated to God by virtue of ordination and are stewards of the mysteries of God in the service of his people. In the pursuit of a life of holiness, clerics are obliged to fulfill their ministry faithfully, nourishing their spiritual life through reading and reflecting on Scripture. The daily celebration of the divine office and regular retreats contribute immensely to a life of holiness. In the Latin Church, clerics are obligated to observe perfect and perpetual continence for the sake of the kingdom of heaven and are therefore bound to observe mandatory celibacy (cc. 277 § 1; 1394 § 1; 1395).

By virtue of their sacred ordination, clerics are prohibited from engaging in certain acts and activities that are incompatible with their vocation. Clerics are therefore "to refrain from establishing or joining associations whose purpose or activity cannot be reconciled with the obligations proper to the clerical state, or which can hinder the diligent fulfillment of the office entrusted them by the competent ecclesiastical authority" (c. 278 § 3). Clerics are not to engage in anything that is unbecoming of their state, in accord with the prescripts of their particular law, nor are they to assume public offices that entail the exercise of civil power (c. 285). Clerics are prohibited, either personally or through others, from engaging in commerce among themselves or others without the express permission of the lawful ecclesiastical authority. Clerics, and particularly priests, are not to be absent from their diocese for any considerable time without the permission of their proper ordinary, or at least his presumed permission (c. 283 § 1). Clerics are not to take part in active partisan politics; nor take any leadership roles in labor unions, nor volunteer for military service without the consent of their lawful ordinary. They may, however, serve as military chaplains with the permission of their proper superior (c. 289 § 1).

Clerics are exhorted to do the following: to be united with one another in the bond of fraternity and prayer to enhance and enrich their pastoral ministry (c. 275 § 1); to acknowledge and promote the vocation of the lay faithful and engage them in the evangelizing mission of the Church in accordance with their state in life (c. 275 § 2); to cultivate a simple lifestyle and to avoid anything that smacks of worldliness (c. 282 § 1); and to foster among the people they serve the observance of peace and harmony based on justice and fairness (c. 287 § 1). Clerics are earnestly recommended to offer the sacrifice of the Eucharist daily (c. 276 § 2; c. 904) and to engage in some kind of communal life to support one another in the ministry.

As members of the Church, clerics have a right to hold ecclesiastical offices for which the power of orders is required. They also have a right to form associations to enhance their ministry and their spiritual well-being (c. 278 § 1). Those clerics who hold ecclesiastical offices are entitled to receive a salary that is in accordance with their condition and the nature and duties of their assignment (c. 281). They have a right to take a sufficient vacation every year. The duration of the vacation is to be decided by the conference of bishops of each country or territory (c. 283 § 2).

If the sacrament of the Holy Orders imprints an indelible character, why then can one lose one's clerical state?

The Church teaches that "sacred ordination once validly received never becomes invalid" (c. 290). However, a validly ordained cleric can lose his clerical state in one of the following ways:

- By a judgment of a competent ecclesiastical court or administrative decree declaring his ordination invalid;
- By the penalty of dismissal, when imposed lawfully; and
- By rescript of the Apostolic See. This rescript is granted only for serious reasons to deacons and very serious reasons for priests (c. 290).

Who are the lay faithful?

The terms "lay faithful" or "laity" as used in this book refers to all the members of the Catholic Church except those in holy orders. Thus, the lay faithful are those members of the Church who, by virtue of their baptism, have been incorporated into the Church. These Church members participate in the common priesthood of Christ and therefore share in the priestly, prophetic, and kingly office of Christ Jesus (*LG*, 31).

The lay faithful, according to the Second Vatican Council, are given a "special vocation to make the Church present and fruitful in those places and circumstances where it is only through them that she (the Church) can become the salt of the earth" (*LG*, 33). The lay faithful, thus, play a special and indispensable role in the evangelizing mission of the Church. Doohan (1984) asserted that the lay faithful should not be seen as belonging "to the Church, nor do they have a role in the Church. Rather, through baptism they are (the) Church, and, in union with Christ, their mission is the mission of the Church itself" (p. 24).

Do the lay faithful have any rights and obligations in the Church?

By virtue of their baptism and confirmation, the lay faithful are accorded certain rights and duties in the Church specific to them, which are listed in canons 224-231 of the *1983 Code of Canon Law.*

The lay faithful have an obligation as individuals and as a group to strive so that the message of the salvation of Jesus Christ may be preached to all nations. Thus, they have a duty to support and participate in the missionary activity of the Church. They are obliged to participate in the evangelizing mission of the Church by permeating and perfecting the temporal order of things with the spirit of God, by becoming the salt of the earth and the light of the world (Mt 5:13-14) in their particular circumstances. The lay faithful, especially those who are married, have a special duty and obligation to strive for the building up of the people of God through their family and married life. Catholic parents have a religious duty to educate and raise their children in the practice of the faith (c. 226).

In addition to these duties and obligations, the lay faithful enjoy a number of rights in the Church (c. 225). They may be allowed by their local ordinary to play certain roles in the Church, such as being a catechist, a judge of a tribunal, a financial administrator, or a member of a diocesan or parish finance council. The lay faithful also have a right to cooperate in the exercise of certain ecclesiastical powers, and this right can be exercised by participating in certain councils. For example, they can participate in diocesan synods and pastoral councils, or they can exercise *in solidum (*together) of the pastoral care of a parish, finance councils, and ecclesiastical tribunals (c. 911). The lay faithful have a right to undergo faith programs to deepen their faith. Thus, the lay faithful have a right to take advanced theological courses at the ecclesiastical universities of the Church to prepare them to participate meaningfully in the teaching office of the Church for the benefit of all. Canon 230 accords the laity the right to perform certain liturgical functions and ministries in the Eucharistic celebration. Thus, they have a right to be lectors, acolytes, cantors, commentators, and extraordinary ministers. Canon 1112 gives the lay faithful a right to assist at marriages in cases of necessity. The lay faithful; who "devote themselves to special service of the Church" (c. 231); have "the right to decent remuneration appropriate to their condition so that they are able to provide decently for their own needs and those of their family" (c. 231 § 2).

Who are the members of the institutes of consecrated life?

Members of the institutes of consecrated life are those Christian faithful, both clergy and laity, who have been consecrated to God and have committed themselves to the saving mission of the Church. Inspired by the Holy Spirit, the members of the institutes of consecrated life try to deepen their baptismal consecration by freely giving their lives to God and thereby committing their lives to the service of God and his Church. Tracing the origin of the institutes of consecrated life in the Church, in *Perfectae caritatis* (October 28, 1965), the Second Vatican Council declared:

> From the very beginning of the Church, there were men and women who set out to follow Christ with greater liberty and to imitate him more closely, by practicing the evangelical counsels. They led lives dedicated to God, each in his own way. Many of them, under the inspiration of the Holy Spirit, became hermits or founded a religious family. (PC, No. 1)

These pious practices were accepted and approved by the competent ecclesiastical authority. The members of the institutes of consecrated life profess the three evangelical counsels of chastity in celibacy, poverty, and obedience. Profession of these evangelical counsels is received by the Church, which recognizes consecrated life as a divine gift and therefore promotes this way of Christian living and supports its members by creating an enabling environment so that members of the Christian faithful may freely assume this lifestyle.

While there are many different institutes of consecrated life in the Church reflecting the diversity of the gifts of the Spirit and different ways of following Christ Jesus, we limit the discussion on the institutes of consecrated life to two: the religious institutes and the secular institutes. The religious life, which is the most traditional form of consecrated life, "was born in the East during the first centuries of Christianity" (*CCC*, 925). Members of the religious life live a common life within religious houses canonically erected by the Church. The elements that distinguish religious life from other forms of consecrated life include:

- Special liturgical worship and commitment of a life of prayer (members develop love for the Holy Mass, the liturgy of the Hours, and common prayers at certain times);
- Public profession of the evangelical counsels by means of perpetual or at least definitive, public vows;
- Fraternal life held in common; and
- Willingness to lead a life of witnessing by separating themselves from the world.

The religious life begins when one is admitted to a novitiate, a period of formation, by the religious superior of the institute, whose responsibility it is to guide the candidate in the process of discernment to ascertain whether he or she has a vocation that requires a religious lifestyle. While in the novitiate, the novices are systematically introduced to the path and demands of a religious life and are formed in the spirit of the religious order. After the completion of the novitiate, those novices judged suitable in accordance with the rules of the institute are admitted to the religious profession. The profession of the three evangelical counsels marks the official entrance into a consecrated life. The profession consists of making the public vows of poverty, chastity, and obedience. The profession of these vows, whether temporary or perpetual, must be received by the legitimate superior.

There are three levels of the governance of religious institutes: governance at the level of the individual religious community or house; governance at the provincial level; and governance at the general level. The governance at each level is administered by a superior who is assisted by council members, whose consent must be obtained when making major decisions. Superiors at each level are elected or appointed for a specific term. Provincial superiors and the superior general are called major superiors. Major decisions affecting the life of the members of the religious institutes are made at a gathering called a *chapter.* In addition to the universal law, each religious institute has its own particular law, statutes, or constitutions, which often inform and direct the conduct of members and spell out the rights and the obligations of members of the institute.

The secular institutes are part of the consecrated institutes whose members live their consecrated lives in the world. Unlike those in the religious life, the members of secular institutes are consecrated to God without abandoning the secular affairs of the world, rather than seek sanctification of earthly realities by their encounters with the secular world. Like members of the religious institutes, members of secular institutes also profess the three evangelical counsels of chastity in celibacy, poverty, and obedience, assuming the three evangelical counsels by means of vows or a sacred bond (promises or an oath). In contrast to the religious life, the common life is not a character of secular institutes. However, members of secular institutes are recommended "to preserve communion among themselves, caring solicitously for a spirit of unity and a genuine relationship as brothers and sisters" (c. 716 § 2).

There is another group of the Christian faithful, the members of societies of apostolic life, who dedicate themselves to an apostolic purpose of the Church. Though members of societies of apostolic life do not make religious vows, they are committed to a fraternal life of community.

CHAPTER 2

Operational Structures of
the Universal Church

What are the basic operational structures of the Catholic Church?

The Catholic Church can be viewed from its universal, diocesan, and parochial structures. The universal Church, which is headed by the Roman Pontiff (the pope) and the College of Bishops, is a communion of particular or diocesan churches. A diocesan church is a communion of a number of parishes or parochial churches. A diocese is "a section of the people of God entrusted to a bishop to be guided by him with the assistance of his clergy so that, loyal to its pastor and formed by him into one community in the Holy Spirit through the Gospel and the Eucharist, it constitutes one particular church in which the one, holy, catholic, and apostolic Church of Christ is truly present and active" (c. 369; Flannery, 1998, p. 569). Canonically, a diocese is called a particular church and the head of a diocesan church is a diocesan bishop. Theological elements in a diocesan church include a diocesan bishop, his presbyterate (his close associates or co-workers), and the people of God. A diocese cannot be erected without the existence of these constitutive elements. For a diocese to be created, it must have its own bishop, who is seen as a focal point of authority in the diocese. Every diocese is required by law to be divided into distinct parts called parishes.

A parish church is "a certain community of the Christian faithful stably constituted in a parish church, whose pastoral care is entrusted to a pastor *(parochus)* as its proper pastor under the authority of the diocesan bishop" (c. 515 § 1). Another canonical name for the pastor of a parish church is a parish priest. The constitutive elements of a parish church are:

(1) a certain community of Christian faithful constituted in a stable manner within a particular church;
(2) its pastoral care entrusted to a pastor or a parish priest as its proper pastor;
(3) it remains only a part of the particular church and never acts as an autonomous entity; and
(4) its proper pastor exercises his pastoral ministry in the parish under the authority of the diocesan bishop.

A parish cannot exist validly in the Catholic Church without a community of Christian faithful or without its proper pastor to whom the pastoral care of the community has been entrusted.

From the aforementioned, one can conclude that there are three most important offices in the Catholic Church: the office of the Bishop of Rome (the pope), the office of a bishop (diocesan or titular), and the office of a parish priest.

Who has the competence to erect, suppress, or alter a parish?

Only the diocesan bishop has the competent authority to erect, suppress, or alter parishes. The diocesan bishop can create a parish only after he has consulted and listened to the advice of his priest council; for otherwise, his actions would be invalid (c. 127 § 2). This consultation is necessary for the validity of his actions, but he is not bound or obliged to follow the counsel of his priest council (c. 500). To erect a parish "means to bring it into existence. To suppress a parish is to end its existence (and) to alter a parish admits a number of possibilities; e.g. to join two or more parishes; to divide a parish into more than one; to change from a territorial to personal or vice versa; to modify parish boundaries" (Beal, Coriden, & Green, 2000, p. 678).

The Supreme Authority of the Church

Jesus clearly stated, "You know that the rulers of nations lord it over them and the leaders have complete authority. It should not be so among you; whoever wants to be more important in your group shall make himself your servant. And whoever wants to be first must make himself the slave of all. Be like the son of man who has come, not to be served but to serve and to give his life to redeem many" (Mk 10:42-45; Mt 20:25-28).

Why then do we still talk about authority in the Church?

The occupants of the various ecclesiastical offices are to serve the common good of the church, preserve its unity, and shepherd the flock, leading and guiding them on their way to salvation. Thus, the authority in the Catholic Church cannot and should not be seen as a relationship of domination, but a relationship of service and love. Reflecting on the ministry of a bishop, Pope Francis (October 24, 2013) reminds newly consecrated bishops that they are ordained to "serve, not to dominate." A bishop or a parish priest is like the head of a family, who is to love the members of his household. Those who hold offices in the Church should care for the people they are ordained to serve. It is because of this understanding that the Church constantly reminds and exhorts her children who are in leadership positions, whether within the Church or in the secular society, to model their leadership styles on that of Jesus Christ, the great leader, who was an example of a servant leader.

Who constitutes the supreme authority in the Church?

The pope and the College of Bishops constitute the supreme authority of the Catholic Church. The pope is the successor of St. Peter and the College of Bishops succeeds the apostolic college (c. 330). The pope and the College of Bishops exercise this authority in the Church when they meet in an ecumenical council. As the head of the College of Bishops, the pope can exercise his authority with or without the College of Bishops. He exercises the authority of his office personally through acts in his own name and through the work of the Roman Curia and his legates who represent him in other countries. The pope also exercises his authority collegially with his brother bishops through ecumenical councils. The College of Bishops possesses supreme and full authority over the universal Church "in solemn manner in an ecumenical council" (c. 337 § 1). The pope decides the way and manner that the College of Bishops exercises its authority collegially over the universal Church.

Who are the members of the College of Bishops?

The College of Bishops is comprised of the validly ordained bishops all over the world who are in hierarchical communion with the Bishop of Rome and other bishops. Thus, to be a member of the College of Bishops, one must:

a. Be a validly ordained bishop. Thus, those, who hold ecclesiastical offices and are equivalent to a diocesan bishop in law, such as an apostolic administrator, a diocesan administrator, a major superior of a religious order, or an abbot who is not a bishop, are not members of the College of Bishops. Retired bishops who are in communion are still members of the College of Bishops. However, a bishop who loses the clerical state (cc. 290-293) is no longer a member of the College of Bishops, even though he remains a validly ordained bishop.
b. Remain in hierarchical communion with the pope and the other members of the College. Thus, a bishop who, due to public heresy, separates himself from communion with the Church is no longer a member of the College.

From the above, one can conclude that there are two principal sources of authority in the Church: the pope acting alone and the College of Bishops acting with the pope. The College of Bishops cannot exercise any supreme authority in the Church without its head, the pope. The pope, being the head of the College of Bishops, has the prerogative to do the following:

a. He can convoke an ecumenical council and preside over it. He can do so personally or through his delegate;
b. He can appoint, remove, transfer, and reinstate bishops; and
c. He can exercise his power any time, with or without the College of Bishops.
d.

As the head of the College of Bishops, the pope enjoys a very special place because of his primacy.

The pope is the Vicar of Christ and the pastor of the universal Church. This means his pastoral role is not limited to the Church in Rome, but to the universal Church. As the supreme pastor of the universal Church, the power of the pope is full; which means that he is the supreme legislator, the supreme judge, and the supreme executor (c. 135). His power to govern the universal Church is immediate, which means that he does not need any intermediaries in order to act. He can involve himself in the governance of any diocese, even against the wishes of the diocesan bishop. It also means that any of the Christian faithful can have access to the pope, and he can deal directly with any member of the Church.

The power of the Servant of the Servants is universal, which means that his power extends to the whole Catholic Church. The power of the Roman Pontiff to govern the universal Church is proper, which means his power is attached to his office and is exercised in his own name. The official titles of the Pope include: the Bishop of Rome, the Vicar of Christ, the successor of Peter, the prince of the apostles, supreme pastor of the universal Church, the Patriarch of the West, archbishop and metropolitan of the Roman Ecclesiastical Province, Sovereign of the State of Vatican City, and Servant of the Servants of God.

Does the authority in the Church have any limits?

The pope and the College of Bishops are bound to exercise the power conferred on them within certain limits for the good of the Church. In exercising their power, the pope and the College of Bishops are limited as to how far they can exercise the power conferred on them. They cannot and must not exercise their power against the purpose of the Church, which is guiding the people of God to reach God and achieve sanctification and salvation. Thus, the goal of authority in the Church is to point the way to God, and it should be exercised in such a way that it will make it much easier for Catholics to achieve sanctification and salvation (Granfield, 1987; Huels, 2001).

The power that Jesus conferred on Peter and the apostles (Mt 16:13-19), which has been transmitted onto the Bishop of Rome and the College of Bishops, is meant to build up and promote unity in the

Church. Thus, in the exercise of legislative, executive, and judicial powers, the pope and his brother bishops should act in such a way that their actions contribute to the unity of faith and the communion of episcopacy. The exercise of authority in the Church is bound to follow the divine natural law; thus, those charged with authority in the Church are to act in accordance with the precepts of the divine natural law. Furthermore, in exercising their powers, the Roman Pontiff and the College of Bishops are to follow the dictates of divine positive law, which is revealed in Sacred Scripture and dogma. This authority cannot and must not be exercised in contradiction to what has been revealed in Scripture and in sacred tradition.

The Holy Father and his brother bishops are to act within the parameters set by canon law; the Church law, to some extent, thus limits their powers. For instance, canon law demands that only celibate men are to be ordained as priests in the Latin Church. No individual bishop can validly ordain a married man to the priesthood. Finally, the power of the Roman Pontiff and the individual bishops is limited to divine revelation. Those charged with power in the Church cannot use it contrary to the dictates of the deposit of faith. For instance, the pope acting alone or with his brother bishops cannot define a doctrine that does not relate to divine revelation.

How does the Bishop of Rome, the pope, govern his diocese?

The diocese of Rome is structured like any large diocese in the world. It has schools, parishes, religious educational programs, a priests' council, a college of consultors, a pastoral council, a seminary for the training and formation of young men for the priesthood, and a cathedral, namely, Saint John Lateran. As a Bishop of Rome, the Holy Father provides pastoral care for the people of God living in his local church. The diocese of Rome is divided into two vicariates: the Vatican vicariate and the Roman vicariate. According to Reese (1996), there is only one parish in the Vatican vicariate, St. Ann's parish, which serves the pastoral needs of the people working in the various departments in Vatican City. Reese maintains that the Roman vicariate has "over 330 parishes with about 450 diocesan and 500 religious priests serving the Catholics living in Rome" (p. 11). The vicar of

Rome, with the assistance of his auxiliary bishops, does the day-to-day pastoral governance of the Roman vicariate.

As a bishop of Rome, the Holy Father is expected to visit parishes in his diocese, interact with parishioners, listen to their concerns and input, and meet with the diocesan priests, who are his close collaborators in the pastoral governance of his diocese. All this must be done in addition to his pastoral duties in the universal Church.

As the supreme pastor, how does the pope govern the universal Church?

As the supreme pastor of the universal Church, the Roman Pontiff governs the Church in collaboration with a number of the people of God, ordained and non-ordained. The Supreme Pontiff "usually conducts the affairs of the universal Church through the Roman Curia, which performs its functions in his name and under his authority for the good and service of the Church. The Roman Curia consists of the Secretariat of State, or the Papal Secretariat, the council for the public affairs of the Church, congregations, tribunals, and other institutes. The constitution and competence of all these are defined in special law" (c. 360).

The Roman Curia: What is it?

The Roman Curia is an institution that assists the Roman Pontiff in handling the various issues that affect the universal Church. The Roman Curia, as we have it today, can be traced through various papal documents that define and structure this institution.

1. In trying to restructure the existing institution, Pope Sixtus V, on January 22, 1588, issued a papal document, *Immensa aeterni Dei,* which reorganized the existing complex papal collaborators to make the existing institution work better. Thus, Pope Sixtus V systemized the work of various congregations, which used to operate in a fragmentary fashion, into a more organized way. Through this papal document, Pope Sixtus V set up the College of Cardinals and other smaller groups to deal with specific issues to promote the unity of the Church.

2. On June 29, 1908, Pope Pius X issued *Sapienti consilio.* Through this papal document, Pope Pius X reorganized the curial departments, as shown in the *1917 Code of Canon Law.*

3. After the Second Vatican Council, Pope Paul VI, on August 15, 1967, issued *Regimini,* which restructured the Curia to reflect emerging themes such as collegiality and the renewed role of the laity, and thus he turned the curial departments to focus more on the service of the Church at the local and universal levels. The document also gave the Roman Curia an international flavor by naming bishops from various parts of the world to head key positions in the Curia and specified five-year terms and age limits for key curial office holders. The *Regimini* gave the Secretariat of State and the Council for Public Affairs very significant roles.

4. On June 28, 1988, Pope John Paul II issued an apostolic constitution, *Pastor bonus.* In this papal document, the Holy Father offered theological and juridical underpinnings for the Roman Curia within the context of ecclesial communion and episcopal collegiality.

What is the purpose of the Roman Curia? How does it assist the pope in the governance of the universal Church?

The main purpose of the Roman Curia, the *Pastor bonus (PB)* maintains, is to serve the Church universally and locally. It also serves individual Christians. Though the Roman Curia is not of divine origin, it is a critical element of the Petrine ministry, because it enables the successor of Peter to effectively safeguard the unity of the Church, serving the College of Bishops, individual bishops, and eventually individual members of the people of God.

The Roman Curia consists of tribunals, congregations, pontifical councils, and other offices. Canonically, these curial agencies are referred to as dicasteries.

Tribunals:

The Roman Curia currently has three tribunals: the Apostolic Penitentiary, the Apostolic Signatura, and the Roman Rota.

The Apostolic Penitentiary (PB, Articles 117-120)

The Apostolic Penitentiary handles excommunication cases reserved to the Holy See. Excommunication cases reserved to the Holy See are: a priest breaking the confessional seal, a priest absolving his accomplice in a sexual sin, a person who physically attacks the Holy Father, a bishop ordaining another bishop and admitting him into episcopacy without the approval of the Holy See, and a person who desecrates the Holy Communion.

This dicastery also handles internal forum cases, whether sacramental or non-sacramental in nature, granting absolutions, dispensations, commutations, validations, condonations, and other favors. The dicastery is also charged with granting the use of indulgences to some extent. The Apostolic Penitentiary deals with very technical cases and its works are done with maximum secrecy.

The Supreme Tribunal of the Apostolic Signatura (PB, Articles 121-125)

The Supreme Tribunal of the Apostolic Signatura is the Supreme Court of the Catholic Church. It functions as the supreme tribunal and ensures that justice prevails in the Church. The Apostolic Signatura has jurisdiction to adjudicate:

1. Complaints of nullity and petitions for total reinstatement against sentences of the Roman Rota;
2. In cases concerning the status of persons, recourse when the Roman Rota has denied a new examination of the case;
3. Exceptions of suspicion and other proceedings against judges of the Roman Rota arising from the exercise of their functions; and
4. Conflicts arising about competence between tribunals that are not subjects of the same appellate tribunal.

The Apostolic Signatura also adjudicates other administrative controversies referred to it by the Roman Pontiff or by the dicasteries of the Roman Curia, as well as conflicts of competence between congregations and pontifical councils. Article 124 of the *Pastor bonus* ascribes the following responsibilities to the Supreme Tribunal of the Apostolic Signatura:

1. To exercise vigilance over the correct administration of justice, and, if need be, to censure advocates and procurators;
2. To deal with petitions to the Roman Rota or other favors relative to the administration of justice; and
3. To grant its approval to the tribunal for appeals reserved to the Holy See and to promote and approve the erection of inter-diocesan tribunals.

The Supreme Tribunal of the Apostolic Signatura is composed of a panel of seven cardinals and four bishops who must have expertise in canon law. The head of the supreme tribunal of the Apostolic Signatura is a cardinal prefect. The staff of the Apostolic Signatura is divided into two sections: the first deals with disputes arising over the jurisdiction between the diocesan tribunals and the procedural appeals from the Roman Rota; the second serves as an administrative tribunal which handles administrative decisions of dicasteries.

The Tribunal of the Roman Rota (PB, Articles 126-127)

The Tribunal of the Roman Rota is a court of higher instance in the Apostolic See. Its main purpose is to safeguard the rights of individuals within the Church, foster the unity of jurisprudence, and provide procedural assistance to lower tribunals. As an appeal court for judicial cases, the Roman Rota handles appeal cases from lower tribunals and first instance cases referred to it by the Roman Pontiff.

Secretariat of State (*PB,* Articles 39-47)

The Secretariat of State, according to *Pastor bonus,* "provides close assistance to the Supreme Pontiff in the exercise of his supreme function" (Article 39). The Secretariat, which is presided over by the Cardinal of the Secretariat of State, contains two sections: the *Section for General Affairs* and the *Section for Relations with States* (PB, Article 40).

In describing the functions of the *Section for General Affairs,* article 41 § 1 of *Pastor bonus* declares that:

It is the task of the First Section (*Section for General Affairs*) in a special way to expedite the business concerning the daily service of the Supreme Pontiff; to deal with those matters which arise outside the ordinary competence of the dicasteries of the Roman Curia and the other institutes of the Apostolic See; to foster relations with those dicasteries and coordinate their work, without prejudice to their autonomy; to supervise the office and work of the legates of the Holy See, especially as concerns the particular churches. This section deals with everything concerning the ambassadors of State to the Holy See.

The *Section for General Affairs* is organized into eight principal languages: English, French, German, Italian, Latin, Portuguese, Spanish, and Polish. In addition to the above-mentioned principal task of the first section, it is also charged to do the following:

1. To draw up and dispatch apostolic constitutions, decretal letters, apostolic letters, epistles, and other documents entrusted to it by the Supreme Pontiff;
2. To prepare the appropriate documents concerning appointments to be made or approved by the Supreme Pontiff in the Roman Curia and in the other institutes depending on the Holy See; and
3. To guard the leaden seal and the fisherman's ring (PB, Article 420).

It is also the responsibility of the first section to "prepare for publication the acts and public documents of the Holy See in the periodical" called *Acta Apostolicae Sedis,* to publish official announcements of acts of the Holy Father or any other activities of the Holy See, and to oversee the official newspaper of the Holy See, *L'Osservatore Romano,* Vatican Radio, and the Vatican Television Center in consultation with the second section.

The competencies of the *Section for Relations with States* include: dealing with the heads of government of various countries, fostering diplomatic relations with civil governments, arranging concordats with states to promote the common interest of the Church, transacting business with the civil government, representing the Holy See at international organizations and meetings concerning questions of a public nature, and dealing with papal legates in matters affecting states (PB, Articles 46 and 47).

Congregations and Pontifical Councils

Currently, there are nine congregations and eleven pontifical councils serving the universal Church under the authority of the Roman Pontiff. Each congregation functions under the headship of a cardinal usually referred to as the "prefect" of the congregation, while the pontifical councils operate under the leadership of a cardinal who is referred to as the "president" of the pontifical council. The prefect of a pontifical congregation or the president of a pontifical council is appointed by the Roman Pontiff for a five-year term which may be renewed.

Though the prefect of a congregation or the president of a pontifical council is in charge of the staff of his respective congregation or council, the day-to-day operation is done by the secretary of the congregation or the council. A secretary of a pontifical congregation is usually an archbishop, whereas the secretary of a pontifical council is a priest with the title of "Monsignor." The secretary of either a congregation or a pontifical council is to have an undersecretary who is a priest and who usually acts like an office manager. In addition, the secretary is to have two or more undersecretaries that may be lay people. Each congregation or council has consultors, who have expertise in the area covered by the congregation or the council. These experts are mostly professors of theology or canon law in Catholic universities, ecclesiastical universities, or pontifical institutes of higher learning all over the world.

The Congregation for the Doctrine of the Faith (PB, Articles 48-55):

The functions and supervision of this dicastery include:
- Fostering and safeguarding the Doctrine of the Faith and morals in the Catholic world. Thus, any matter touching on faith and moral issues falls within the jurisdiction of the Congregation for the Doctrine of the Faith;
- Examining and condemning heretical writings that threaten the core elements of the Catholic faith;

- Reviewing curial documents that touch on faith and morals; and
- Being in charge of the Pontifical Biblical Commission and the International Theological Commission.

The Congregation for the Eastern Catholic Churches (PB, Articles 56-61):

- This congregation has jurisdiction over all matters that are proper to the Eastern Catholic Churches. It is in charge of missionary activities in Eastern territories.

The Congregation for Divine Worship and the Discipline of the Sacraments (PB, Articles 62-70):

- Prepares and revises all the liturgical books and grants the *recognitio* to translations and adaptations of liturgical books prepared by the conferences of bishops;
- Handles cases pertaining to the nullity of ordination and the laicization of clergy, and cases of the non-consummation of marriages;
- Reviews particular calendars and liturgical texts for particular churches and religious institutes; and
- Handles matters relating to relics and the confirmation of patron saints, granting the title of minor basilica.

The Congregation for the Causes of Saints (PB, Articles 71-74):

- Handles cases of canonization and beatification, granting authenticity to relics and handling their preservation; and is
- Charged with the investigation leading to granting the title "Doctors of the Church."

The Congregation for Bishops (PB, Articles 75-84):

- Examines and supervises the creation and provision of particular churches, and oversees the exercise of the conferences of bishops in the Latin Church;

- Deals with everything that pertains to the constitution, division, union, suppression, and other changes of particular churches and their groupings. It has the competence to erect military ordinariates for the pastoral care of the members of armed forces;
- Handles everything concerning the appointment of bishops, even titular ones, and generally, the creation of particular churches;
- Organizes the *ad limina* visits;
- Has jurisdiction over everything involving the Holy See in matters of personal prelatures;
- Deals with matters pertaining to the celebration of particular councils as well as the creation of the bishops' conference and granting *recognitio* to their statutes; and
- Is in-charge of the pontifical commission for Latin America.

The Congregation for the Evangelization of Peoples (PB, Articles 85-92):

- Handles missionary activity, except in the territories of the Eastern Catholic Churches;
- Engages in positive programs to awaken missionary vocations, whether clerical, religious, or lay, and advises on the suitable distribution of missionaries;
- Handles the education of secular clergy and of catechists in mission territories; and
- Deals with the missionaries of the societies of apostolic life.

The Congregation for the Clergy (PB, Articles 93-104):

- Has competence over matters concerning the life, conduct, rights, and obligations of the clergy;
- Handles matters that promote vocations to the priesthood and seminary education;
- Handles the establishment of inter-diocesan seminaries and approval of their statutes;
- Deals with all matters affecting priests and deacons of the secular clergy;

- Deals with matters concerning presbyteral councils, colleges of consultors, pastoral councils, parishes, churches, shrines, clerical associations, and ecclesiastical archives, or records;
- Deals with matters concerning the suitable distribution of priests;
- Handles Mass obligations, pious wills, and pious foundations; and
- Handles questions concerning the temporal goods of the Church.

The Congregation for Institutes of Consecrated Life and for Societies of Apostolic Life (PB, Articles 105-111):

- Promotes and supervises in the whole Latin Church, the practice of the evangelical counsels as they are practiced by the members of the institutes of consecrated life and societies of apostolic life;
- Deals with the erection, suppression, and approval of the constitutions of the institutes of consecrated life and societies of apostolic life;
- Handles all matters affecting the institutes of consecrated life and societies of apostolic life and their members, including formation, government, apostolate, rights, and obligations, dispensation from vows, dismissal, and the administration of goods; and
- Deals with the establishment and approval of statutes and the activities of the conferences of the major superiors.

The Congregation for Catholic Education (PB, Articles 112-116):

- Deals with matters pertaining to Catholic schools; and
- Handles Catholic universities and other higher education institutes.

The Pontifical Council for the Laity (PB, Articles 131-134):

The Pontifical Council for the Laity has jurisdiction over the following:

- The apostolate and Christian life of the lay people, supporting the lay people's participation in the life and mission of the Church in their own way; and
- Dealing with the erection and approval of statutes of the international lay associations of the faithful, except for the third orders and associations intending to become institutes of consecrated life or societies of apostolic life.

The Pontifical Council for Promoting Christian Unity (PB, Articles 135-138):

- This council brings together and coordinates national and international Catholic organizations with the aim of promoting Christian unity; and
- Deals with matters concerning ecumenism, issuing documents that promote dialogues with the Jewish people.

The Pontifical Council for the Family (PB, Articles 139-141):

- Handles matters pertaining to the pastoral care of families, protecting the rights and dignity of the family in the Church and in civil society;
- Effectively promotes a deeper understanding of the Church's teachings on the family; and
- Encourages studies in the spirituality of marriages and family life.

The Pontifical Council for Justice and Peace (PB, Articles 142-144):

- Handles all matters pertaining to the promotion of human rights and justice;
- Collects and handles information and research on justice and peace, human development, and violations of fundamental human rights; and

- Deals with matters that foster peace and is in charge of preparing the celebration of World Peace Day.

The Pontifical Council *Cor Unum* (PB, Articles 145-148):

- This council encourages and shares the solicitude of the Catholic Church for the needy, thereby promoting human fraternity among all. Its principal functions include:

  o Stimulating the Christian faithful to be participants in the mission of the Church by giving witness to evangelical charity;
  o Fostering and coordinating the initiatives of Catholic institutions that work to help people in need; and
  o Giving serious attention to and promoting plans to undertake joint actions that serve human progress.

The Pontifical Council for the Pastoral Care of Migrant/Itinerant People (PB, Articles 149-151):

- Handles all pastoral initiatives that promote the spiritual well-being of migrants; and
- Encourages the particular churches to see to it that refugees, exiles, migrants, nomads, and workers residing within their respective local churches are given the care they need.

The Pontifical Council for Pastoral Assistance to Healthcare Workers (PB, Articles 152-143):

- Encourages and supports healthcare professionals in their work with the sick and suffering by providing them with the necessary spiritual background;
- Promotes the Church's teachings on the spiritual and moral aspects of illness as well as the meaning of human suffering; and
- Deals with matters that enable healthcare workers to get the spiritual care they need as they carry out their work in accordance with Christian teachings.

The Pontifical Council for the Interpretation of Legislative Texts (PB, Articles 154-158):

- Handles all matters pertaining to the publication of the authentic interpretation of the universal laws of the Church which are confirmed by pontifical authority;
- Reviews the general executory decrees and instructions of the Roman dicasteries to ensure that they are in conformity with the prescription of the law currently in force and that they are drawn up in the correct juridical form; and
- Reviews the decrees of the conferences of bishops before the competent dicastery grants the *recognitio.*

The Pontifical Council for Inter-Religious Dialogue (PB, Articles 159-162):

- Handles matters concerning the promotion of healthy relations between the Catholic Church and non-Christian religions.

The Pontifical Council for Dialogue with non-Believers (PB, Articles 163-165):

- Promotes the study of atheism and reasons for the lack of faith and religion, investigating the causes and their consequences with regard to the Christian faith, so that suitable assistance may be given, and especially pastoral action, through the work of Catholic institutions of higher learning.

The Pontifical Council for Culture (PB, Articles 166-168):

- Promotes relations between the Holy See and the realm of human culture by encouraging discussion with various contemporary institutions of learning and teachings so that secular cultures may be more open to the Gospel message.

The Pontifical Council for Social Communication (PB, Articles 169-170):

- Handles all matters concerning social communication; and
- Reviews Catholic newspapers and periodicals as well as radio and television stations, so that they will truly live up to their nature and function, by transmitting the teachings of the Church.

The Pontifical Council for Promoting New Evangelization (UBS, Articles 1-4):

On January 16, 2013, the Holy Father, Pope Benedict XVI, established an additional pontifical council, pontifical council for promoting new evangelization, as a dicastery of the Roman Curia in compliance with the Apostolic Constitution, *Pastore bonus.* This new council has the following responsibilities:
- Handles topics relating to the new evangelization and identifies suitable ways and means to accomplish it;
- The specific tasks of the council include:
  o Examining the theological and pastoral meaning of the new evangelization in depth;
  o Promoting and fostering, in close collaboration with the bishops' conferences, the study, dissemination, and implementation of the Papal Magisterium related to topics connected with the new evangelization;
  o Publicizing and supporting initiatives linked to the new evangelization that are already being put into practice in various particular churches and to promoting the realization of new projects by actively involving the resources present in the institutes of consecrated life and in the societies of apostolic life, as well as in groups of the faithful and in new communities;
  o Studying and encouraging the use of modern forms of communication as instruments of the new evangelization; and
  o Promoting the use of the *Catechism of the Catholic Church* as an essential and complete formulation of the content of the faith for the people of our time (Article 3, Numbers 1-5).

Papal Offices

In addition to the tribunals, congregations, and pontifical councils, the Roman Curia has important offices that exercise vital functions assigned to them by a special law. These offices are:

The Office of the Apostolic Camera

This office is presided over by the cardinal chamberlain of the Holy Catholic Church, who is assisted by the vice-chamberlain and other prelates of the camera. This office exercises a special role during the vacancy of the Apostolic See. The *Pastor bonus* maintains that "when the Apostolic See falls vacant, it is the right and the duty of the cardinal chamberlain of the Holy Roman Church, personally or through his delegate, to request, from all administrations dependent on the Holy See, reports on their patrimonial and economic status as well as information on any extraordinary business that may at that time be under way, and from the prefecture for the Economic Affairs of the Holy See, he shall request a financial statement on the income and expenditures of the previous year and budgetary estimates for the following year. He is obliged to submit these reports and estimates to the College of Cardinals" (Article 171).

The Office of the Administration of the Patrimony of the Apostolic See

This office "administers the properties owned by the Holy See in order to provide the funds necessary for the Roman Curia to function" (PB, Article 172). This office is presided over by a cardinal, who is assisted by a board of cardinals. The office is composed of two sections: the ordinary section and the extraordinary section. The ordinary section "examines matters regarding the juridical and economic status of the employees of the Holy See; it supervises institutions under its fiscal responsibility; it sees to the provision of all that is required to carry out the ordinary business and specific aims of the dicasteries; it maintains records of income and expenditures, prepares an account of the money received and paid out for the past year, and draws up the estimates for the year to come" (Article 174).

The extraordinary section administers moveable goods and acts entrusted to it by the Holy See.

The Office of the Papal Household

The office of the papal household consists of dignitaries who assist the Roman Pontiff in carrying out certain important ceremonies of either religious or civil character. The papal household is divided into two sections: the papal chapel and the papal family.

The papal chapel consists of dignitaries who help the pope in carrying out religious ceremonies as a spiritual leader of the Church. The papal family consists of dignitaries who assist the pope in exercising his civil functions as the head of a juridical body.

The office of the papal household looks after the internal arrangement of the papal household and supervises everything related to the conduct and services of all clerics and laypersons that make up the papal chapel and papal family. The office is in the service of the pope at his palace and when he travels. It is the duty of this office to arrange public and private audiences with the pope. The office is, thus, in constant consultation with the Secretariat of State regarding the appropriate procedures to follow when the pope is to meet with heads of states, ambassadors, members of governments, public authorities, and other dignitaries.

The Office for the Liturgical Celebrations of the Supreme Pontiff

The office for the liturgical celebrations prepares all that is necessary for the liturgical and other sacred celebrations performed by the pope or by his delegate and supervises them in accordance with the current prescriptions of liturgical law. The office is headed by the master of papal liturgical celebrations, who is appointed for a five-year term.

Papal Legates

Another important institution that, although not part of the Roman Curia, plays a critical role in the pastoral ministry of the Roman Pontiff to the universal Church is the institution of papal legates.

Who are the papal legates? How do they assist in the governance of the universal Church?

The papal legates are senior clergymen "entrusted with the office of representing the Roman Pontiff in a stable manner to particular churches or also the states and public authorities where they are sent" (c. 363). There are two forms of papal representation: the nunciature and the apostolic delegation.

The nunciature is headed by a nuncio or apostolic nuncio. The nuncio serves in a country that has diplomatic relations with the Holy See as both the ambassador of the Holy See and as the representative of the Holy Father to a local church in his host nation. Thus, the apostolic nuncio deals with the critical issues facing the local church in his host nation as well as political and social issues confronting the civil government of the country to which he is accredited. The nuncio also concerns himself with the relationship between the state and the Church.

The apostolic delegation is non-diplomatic representation of the Holy Father at international organizations such as UN, FAO, and UNESCO. The Holy Father sends delegates, clerics, or laypersons to represent him at international organizations or conferences. These papal representatives are called delegates when the Holy See is a permanent member of the organization to which they are sent; otherwise; they are referred to as observers.

The duties of papal legates are categorized into ecclesiastical duties and diplomatic responsibilities. The ecclesiastical duties of papal legates are:

a. Send information to the Apostolic See concerning the conditions of particular churches and everything that touches the life of the church and the good of souls;
b. Assist the bishops by action and counsel, but do not interfere in the legislative power of the bishops;
c. Foster close relations with the bishops' conference by offering assistance to it in every way;
d. Assist in the process of nominating a local bishop by verifying the suitability of the candidate to be named bishop;
e. Promote matters which pertain to peace, progress, and the cooperative efforts of people;

f. Collaborate with the local bishops so that suitable relations are fostered between the Catholic Church and other churches or ecclesial communities, even with non-Christian religions;

g. Work with the local bishops to promote the mission of the Church and the Apostolic See and

h. Exercise their duties and fulfill other mandates which the Apostolic See entrusts to them. (c. 364)

The diplomatic responsibilities of the papal legates are:

a. Promoting and fostering relations between the Apostolic See and the authorities of the states;

b. Dealing with questions that pertain to relations between the Church and the state; and

c. Dealing with the drafting and implementing of concordats and other agreements of this type in a special way (c. 365).

Does the Roman Pontiff have any consultative bodies?

Like any other leader of a large organization or institution, the Roman Pontiff has a number of people who assist and counsel him on a number of issues. This discussion is limited to two: the Synod of Bishops and the College of Cardinals.

What is the Synod of Bishops?

The Synod of Bishops is "a group of bishops who have been chosen from different regions of the world and meet together at fixed times to foster closer unity between the Roman Pontiff and bishops, to assist the Roman Pontiff with their counsel in the preservation and growth of faith and morals and in the observance and strengthening of ecclesiastical discipline, and to consider questions pertaining to the activity of the Church in the world" (c. 342).

Pope Paul VI created the Synod of Bishops on September 14, 1965, in his *Motu proprio, Apostolica sollicitudo,* as a consultative organ for the Roman Pontiff in an effort to promote collegiality among his brother bishops. The three types of Synods of Bishops are:

1. The ordinary general assembly;

2. The extraordinary general assembly; and
3. The special synod (c. 345).

The ordinary general assembly and the extraordinary general Synod
of Bishops deal with matters affecting the universal Church, while
the special Synod of Bishops deals with matters affecting particular
churches in a particular geographical region or regions.

The *Apostolica sollicitudo* tasks the general Synod of Bishops with
the following functions:

a. Promoting a closer union and greater cooperation between the
    Supreme Pontiff and the bishops of the whole world;
b. Seeing to it that accurate and direct information is supplied
    on matters and situations that bear upon the internal life of the
    Church and upon the kinds of actions that should be carried out
    in today's world; and
c. Facilitating agreement among essential matters of doctrine and
    the course of actions to be taken by the Church (*AS, 1*).

The pope sets limits on how far the Synod of Bishops can go in
its deliberation of issues confronting the universal Church or particular
churches in a given region, thereby distinguishing the Synod of
Bishops from the College of Bishops. The duty of the Synod of
Bishops is to discuss and deliberate on issues it is tasked to discuss
and to propose recommendations to the Supreme Pontiff. A Synod of
Bishops lacks the jurisdiction to make decisions or draw up decrees
on matters it was set to discuss, unless the Supreme Pontiff expressly
grants the synod the mandate to do so.

A Synod of Bishops is convoked to give information and counsel
to the Roman Pontiff. The final recommendations of the Synod of
Bishops are given in the name of the pope, not the Synod. A Synod
of Bishops is, therefore, a personal exercise of papal power and never
a collegial power. A Synod of Bishops is subject to the control and
authority of the pope directly. He alone does the following:

a. Convokes a Synod of Bishops as often as it seems opportune to
    him and designates the place where its sessions are to be held;

b. Ratifies (or vetoes) the selection of members who must be elected according to the norms of a special law and designates and appoints other members;

c. At an appropriate time before gathering a synod, determines the contents of the questions to be discussed, according to the norms of a special law;

d. Defines the agenda;

e. Presides at the synod personally or through others; and

f. Concludes, transfers, suspends, and dissolves the synod (c. 344; *Apostolica sollicitudo,* III).

The following are examples of ordinary general Synods of Bishops:

1967 Synod of Bishops dealt with challenges to the faith, revision of the code of canon law, seminaries, and liturgical reform;

1971 Synod of Bishops addressed the ministerial priesthood and justice in the world;

1974 Synod of Bishops dealt with issues of evangelization in the modern world;

1977 Synod of Bishops focused on the importance of catechesis;

1980 Synod of Bishops treated the Christian family;

1983 Synod of Bishops treated penance and reconciliation;

1987 Synod of Bishops treated the vocation and mission of the lay faithful;

1990 Synod of Bishops treated the formation of priests;

1994 Synod of Bishops studied the consecrated life and its role in the Church and the world;

2001 Synod of Bishops studied the topic of the bishop-servant of the Gospel of Jesus Christ, the Hope of the World (Huels, 2001); and

2012 Synod of Bishops studied the new evangelization for the transmission of the Christian faith.

In 1969, the extraordinary general assembly treated the issues of collegiality, the conferences of bishops, and the revision of the *Code of Canon Law,* while the 1985 extraordinary general assembly explored the reformed liturgy and the theology of *communion.*

A special assembly, which normally treats matters affecting the particular churches in a given geographical region or regions, is often called to investigate issues affecting some particular churches. Some examples of such special Synods of Bishops are:

1980 Special Synod of Bishops on the Church in the Netherlands;
1991 Special Synod of Bishops on the Church in Europe;
1994 Special Synod of Bishops on the Church in Africa;
1995 Special Synod of Bishops on the Church in Lebanon;
1998 Special Synod of Bishops on the Church in Asia; and
2009 Special Synod on the Church in Africa.

The College of Cardinals: What is it? How did it originate in the Church?

The College of Cardinals is another important consultative organ of the Supreme Pontiff. The word "cardinal" comes from the Latin word "cardo," which is translated as the "hinge" that holds the door. In the early church, a cleric was ordained for a particular office for life. The position was given to the cleric as his "title" and the cleric was called the "titular" of the position for which he was ordained for life. If, for any reason, the cleric switched to another position or office for which he was not ordained, he was said to have been incardinated in the latter position and was called the "cardinal" of the new position he had taken.

Some clerics, because of some outstanding qualities, talents, and gifts that they had, were transferred to other positions for the common good of the Church, and these transferred clerics became "cardinals" instead of "titulars" of their new positions. The increasing demand for gifted and talented clerics to assist at the liturgical services at the major shrines of martyrs, such as the basilicas of Saint Peter's, St. John Lateran, St. Paul Outside the Wall, and St. Mary Major, fuelled the practice of transferring talented and outstanding clerics from the original posts for which they were ordained to assist at these shrines and basilicas, thus changing them from being "titulars" to "cardinals" at these shrines and basilicas. This practice of transferring gifted and talented clerics from different areas to Rome to assist at the major shrines of martyrs and basilicas gave birth to the cardinal priests (cardinals of presbyteral order) we have in the College of Cardinals. These cardinals serve in different major archdioceses all over the world.

The gifted and talented bishops of suburban towns around the city of Rome were also invited to perform some episcopal services at St. John Lateran Basilica, the cathedral church of the diocese of Rome. While retaining the positions for which they were ordained as "titulars," they became "cardinals" when assisting at St. John Lateran Church as bishops. In addition to assisting at the cathedral church, these bishops were consulted with by the Bishop of Rome on a number of issues affecting the local Church in Rome. This practice of bishops from the suburban towns assisting at St. John Lateran and advising the Bishop of Rome as "cardinals," that is, in their new positions, is the origin of the cardinal bishops in the College of Cardinals. The cardinal bishops are attached to the seven suburbicarian (the major) sees around Rome.

As the pope assumed the civil governance of Rome, there was a greater need for deacons to provide social services at different centers in Rome. The main task of the deacons at these centers was to care for the poor and to provide for their needs. The deacons at these centers also advised the popes on their pastoral ministry to the poor and the marginalized and on social service policies in general. The ministry of the deacons at these centers gave rise to the present-day cardinal deacons in the College of Cardinals.

Reese (1996) maintained that since the clerics chosen for the functions mentioned above were normally more talented, gifted, and outstanding in their ministry, it was natural that they became advisers to the popes. From the aforementioned, one can clearly see three distinct ranks in the College of Cardinals: the cardinal priests (the presbyteral order), the cardinal bishops (the episcopal order) and the cardinal deacons (the diaconal order).

Pope Leo IX (1049-54) was the first to name cardinals from outside the area of Rome. These cardinals resigned their positions and took up residence in Rome. Pope Nicholas II decreed in 1059 that cardinals were to elect the Bishop of Rome, and at the third Lateran Council in 1179, Pope Alexander III decreed that the election of the Supreme Pontiff is the exclusive right of the College of Cardinals and that a two-thirds majority of the cardinals was required to elect the Bishop of Rome (*UDG*, 70).

In 1962, Pope John XXIII ordained all cardinals who were not bishops to the order of episcopacy. Thus, since 1962, all cardinals must be bishops. However, one may be dispensed of episcopal ordination if one is already eighty years old. The three distinct ranks in the College of Cardinals: cardinal priest, cardinal bishop, and cardinal deacon are now only honorific titles.

The cardinal bishops are assigned to the seven titular sees, which are: Ostia, Albano, Frascati, Palestrina, Porto-Santa Ruffina, Sabina-Poggio Mireto, and Velletri-Segni. The patriarchs of the Eastern Catholic Churches who are cardinals retain their patriarchal sees as their titles and their rank as cardinal bishops in the College of Cardinals. The cardinal priests are given the title of a Church in Rome, while each of the cardinal deacons is assigned one of the diaconal centers that used to be staffed by deacons in the early Church. As of February 28, 2013, there were 10 cardinal bishops, 44 cardinal deacons, and 153 cardinal priests. Four of the ten cardinal bishops are patriarchs in Eastern Catholic Churches. Generally, cardinal priests are archbishops of large archdioceses all over the world, while the cardinal bishops and cardinal deacons are curial officials who are residents of Rome.

What are the functions of the College of Cardinals?

The principal functions of the College of Cardinals are "to elect the pope in accordance with the norms of a special law and they do so in a conclave, to assist the Supreme Pontiff in his task as a universal pastor. They assist the pope collegially when they are summoned in consistory or individually through different offices the cardinals discharge" (c. 353).

There are two types of consistory: ordinary consistory and extraordinary consistory or general congregation. The ordinary consistory deals with serious, but recurring matters, affecting the Church or carries out some solemn celebration, such as the creation of new cardinals or the canonization of a saint in the Church. All the cardinals who reside in Rome are invited to the ordinary consistory. The public, that is the prelates, representatives of civil societies, and the general public, are invited to the ordinary (c. 353 § 2).

The extraordinary consistory, or general congregation, on the other hand, addresses matters that are even more serious, like some special pastoral concerns or organizational and governmental needs of the Church. An extraordinary consistory may also be called to advise the Supreme Pontiff on more serious and pressing issues affecting the universal Church. All cardinals are invited to attend an extraordinary consistory.

What are the structures of the College of Cardinals?

The College of Cardinals has the following organs: dean of the college, sub-dean of the college, cardinal camerlengo, cardinal proto-deacon, and secretary of the college. The dean of cardinals presides over the College of Cardinals. He is the ceremonial head of the college and does not possess any power of governance over the other cardinals. He is only seen as first among equals. The dean is chosen from among the members of the cardinal bishops who have the suburbicarian titles. The dean of the College of Cardinals has the title of the Church of Ostia (c. 350 § 4). His principal duties include:

a. Notifying the cardinals, the diplomatic body, and the heads of states of the death of the Roman Pontiff;
b. Convoking general congregations of the College of Cardinals and the conclave;
c. Ordaining the newly elected pope a bishop, if he is not already a bishop;
d. Presiding over the meeting of the College of Cardinals, if the pope is absent or impeded; and
e. Addressing the concerns of the cardinals and any questions arising within the College of Cardinals.

The sub-dean of the College of Cardinals has juridical status similar to the dean of cardinals. He assumes the duties of the dean if the dean is absent or impeded. The cardinal camerlengo is chosen from among the college. He presides over the apostolic camera and remains in office if the Bishop of Rome dies. His main duty is to supervise and administer the goods and rights of the Holy See, in general, and of the Roman Curia.

The cardinal proto-deacon is the most senior cardinal from the diaconal order. He announces the name of the newly elected pope to the world. He also fills in for the pope, when he is impeded, in conferring the pallium on the archbishops and their proxies (c. 355 § 2). The Secretary of the Congregation for Bishops performs the secretarial duties of the College of Cardinals.

CHAPTER 3

Particular Churches and Their Groupings

What does the term "particular church" mean?

The term "particular church," as used in the *1983 Code of Canon Law*, refers to all dioceses and other kinds of gatherings of the Catholic faithful: territorial prelatures, territorial abbacies, apostolic vicariates, apostolic prefectures, apostolic administrations, and military ordinariates. In other words, the term "particular church" is another name for a "diocese" and other groupings of the Catholic faithful. The head of a diocese is a diocesan bishop. The people who head these other particular churches are equivalent in law to a diocesan bishop, even if they have not received episcopal ordination. Particular churches may have territorial boundaries, such as dioceses, or they may be without territorial boundaries, like military ordinariates. All of the Catholic faithful within the limits of a particular church constitute one local church in the overarching Church of Christ.

As the successor of St. Peter, the Roman Pontiff is the visible source and foundation of the unity between both the bishops and the Catholic faithful. Similarly, the individual diocesan bishops and those equivalent in law to a diocesan bishop "are the visible source and foundation of unity in their own particular churches, which are constituted after the model of the universal Church. It is in these and formed out of them that the one and unique Catholic Church exists" (*LG*, 23). A diocesan bishop is the central figure in the local church that has been entrusted to his pastoral care. This is also true for the heads of other particular churches mentioned in canon 368.

The office of bishop in the Catholic Church is of divine origin and confers the powers to sanctify, teach, and govern in the name of Christ

Jesus. These powers are to be exercised in hierarchical communion with the Bishop of Rome and other members of the College of Bishops (c. 375). Bishops in the Catholic Church possess the fullness of the holy orders (*LG*, 26).

A priest becomes a bishop through episcopal ordination. Episcopal ordination and canonical mission, which is given by the Supreme Pontiff, are critical in the valid functions of a bishop. Episcopal ordination confers an ontological share on the bishop so that he can exercise his ministry as a bishop. The canonical mission confers the hierarchical authority that the bishop needs to govern his diocese in communion with the Bishop of Rome and the other members of the College of Bishops.

What are the required qualifications for the office of a bishop?

To be suitable for the office of a bishop, a priest must be:

1. Outstanding in faith, morals, piety, zeal for souls, wisdom, prudence, and human virtues, and endowed with other qualities that make him suitable to fulfill the office in question;
2. Of good reputation;
3. At least thirty-five years old;
4. Ordained to the presbyterate for at least five years; and
5. In possession of a doctorate or a licentiate in sacred Scripture, theology, or canon law from an institute of higher studies approved by the Apostolic See or at least is truly expert in the same discipline (c. 378).

The final and definitive decision on the suitability of a candidate to be promoted to the order of a bishop rests with the Apostolic See. A bishop is either a diocesan bishop or titular bishop. A diocesan bishop is one to whom the pastoral care of a diocese has been entrusted, for instance, the Archbishop of New York. Any other bishop, that is, one who has not been entrusted with the pastoral care of a specific diocese, is a titular bishop.

How does a priest become a bishop in the Church?

Every three years, bishops of every ecclesiastical province are required to prepare a list of priests (*terna*) they view as suitable for the office of bishop. This list is sent to the Apostolic See through the office of the papal legate (c. 377 § 2). The papal legate may also do his own investigation regarding the suitability of the candidates before sending the *terna* to the Apostolic See with his comments and suggestions (c. 377 § 3).

The Roman Pontiff freely appoints from the *terna* after listening to the people of a given ecclesiastical province or country through his legate. The Holy Father may choose a priest to be a bishop apart from the terna. In other instances where the local church has the legitimate right to elect a candidate for the episcopate, the Supreme Pontiff confirms the candidate that has been legitimately elected by the priests of a given diocese. The procedure for appointing a bishop includes the following, in this order:

1. An individual priest is judged to be suitable for the episcopacy;
2. The pope freely appoints him to the episcopacy or confirms him when he is elected;
3. The priest receives episcopal ordination by at least three bishops; and
4. The newly ordained bishop takes canonical possession of his office as a diocesan, coadjutor, or auxiliary bishop.

What does the term "pastoral governance" mean?

In his diocese, a diocesan bishop possesses all the ordinary, proper, and immediate power needed to function as the chief pastor (c. 381 § 1). As a vicar of Christ in his diocese, the diocesan bishop exercises his powers of governance in the name of Christ. His power of governance is sacred and personal, because it comes from his episcopal ordination; however, it becomes juridical power through the canonical mission he receives from the Bishop of Rome. Canon 391 § 1 distinguishes the diocesan bishop's power of governance as legislative, executive, and judicial. He exercises these pastoral powers to govern his diocese. The power of a diocesan bishop is ordinary, which means his power is attached to his office as a diocesan bishop. His power is proper, which means his power is exercised in his own name as a vicar of Christ in his diocese. Finally, his power is immediate, which means that he can involve himself in the governance of any parish within his diocese in accordance with the dictates of canon law. It also means that any Catholic faithful in the diocese can have access to the bishop, who can deal directly with the people of God in any parish church.

In governing his diocese, a diocesan bishop must not discriminate against any of the people in his local church, but must show "concern for all the Christian faithful entrusted to his care," regardless of race, tribe, age, or nationality. He must "act with humility and charity toward the brothers and sisters who are not in full communion with the Catholic Church and is to foster ecumenism as it is understood by the Church" (c. 383 § 3).

As an authentic teacher of the faith, a diocesan bishop has a duty to explain the tenets of the Catholic faith to the people of God in his diocese. He also encourages and supervises the strict observation of "the prescripts of the canons on the ministry of the word, especially those on homily and catechetical instruction" (c. 736). He has the right to preach the Word of God everywhere in his diocese. He also has a duty to issue norms for catechesis, making sure that modern instruments are available to facilitate religious instruction and formation.

In exercising his sanctifying duty, a diocesan bishop has an obligation to "show an example of holiness in charity, humility, and simplicity of life. He is to strive to promote in every way the holiness of the Christian faithful according to the proper vocation of each"(c. 387).

How does diocesan curia assist the diocesan bishop in the governance of his diocese?

Governing a diocese is an immense responsibility, and as such, the diocesan bishop cannot fulfill these responsibilities alone. He needs the assistance of other people. A diocesan curia assists a diocesan bishop in the pastoral governance of his diocese. A diocesan curia consists of those offices that assist a diocesan bishop in exercising his threefold *munera* (functions) of teaching, sanctifying, and governing.

A diocesan curia is made up of "those institutions and persons which assist the bishop in the governance of the whole diocese, especially in guiding pastoral action, in caring for the administration of the diocese, and in exercising judicial power" (c. 469). The diocesan curia is a complex entity, composed of many offices, linked together to assist the diocesan bishop in the pastoral governance of his local church. Thus, the principal function of a diocesan curia is to assist the diocesan bishop in studying, planning, and carrying out pastoral programs together with his priests' council and pastoral council, if the latter exists in his diocese.

The diocesan bishop freely names those he considers suitable to the various offices in his curia. Those appointed to positions in the curia must promise to fulfill their functions faithfully, according to the manner determined by law or by the diocesan bishop and to observe secrecy within the limits and according to the manner determined by law or by the diocesan bishop. The universal law requires the diocesan curia to have certain mandated offices, while other offices are optional. The mandated offices are: vicar general, episcopal vicar (depending on the size of the diocese), judicial vicar, chancellor, financial administrator, finance council, ecumenical commission, and liturgical commission. A diocesan bishop may also include any of the following to his curia: a diocesan pastoral council, catechetical office, social affairs office, Catholic charities, and education office.

The office of the vicar general and episcopal vicar: Is the diocesan bishop required by law to appoint a vicar general and episcopal vicar?

Every diocesan bishop must appoint a vicar general to assist him in the pastoral governance of his diocese. The diocesan bishop may appoint an episcopal vicar or vicars, depending on the size of the diocese. The vicar general has ordinary powers attached to his office. His power is, however, vicarious, that is, he exercises it in the name of the diocesan bishop (c. 475).

The vicar general must be a priest who is at least thirty years old at the time of his appointment, with a doctorate or licentiate in canon law, theology, or sacred Scripture, or who is at least an expert in these disciplines and is known for his sound doctrine, integrity, prudence, and practical experience. The power of the episcopal vicar, unlike the vicar general, is limited to some specific parts of the diocese, or to a specific group of people.

If the vicar general or episcopal vicar is not a bishop, he loses his office when:

1. The term for which he was appointed has expired, and he has received notification of that fact in writing from the diocesan bishop;
2. He resigns from office after he reaches the retirement age and his resignation has been accepted by the diocesan bishop;
3. He is removed from office by the diocesan bishop (the vicar general can be removed from office for any just cause); or
4. The See becomes vacant by the death of the bishop, his resignation, or his transfer to another diocese (c. 481).

What does the term "local ordinary" mean?

Canonically, the term "local ordinary" refers to the Roman Pontiff, a diocesan bishop, a diocesan administrator, an apostolic administrator, the head of a territorial prelature, territorial abbacy, apostolic vicariate, or apostolic prefecture, or anyone who possesses general ordinary executive power, such as a vicar general or episcopal vicar (c. 134 § 1).

The term "ordinary" refers to all those persons mentioned above and the major superiors of clerical religious institutes and clerical societies of apostolic life of pontifical right who possess and exercise ordinary executive powers. The major superiors of clerical religious institutes and societies of apostolic life of pontifical right are often referred to as *personal ordinaries* (c. 134).

Who is a judicial vicar?

The universal law of the Church requires every bishop to appoint a judicial vicar who constitutes one tribunal with the bishop. The judicial vicar cannot judge cases that the diocesan bishop reserves for himself (c. 1420). The judicial vicar must be a priest with a good reputation, must hold a doctorate or at least a licentiate in canon law, and must not be less than thirty years of age.

What are the functions of the diocesan chancellor?

The chancellor is the chief notary and the chief secretary of the diocesan curia. As a chief secretary, the chancellor countersigns all the official documents of the diocesan bishop and the vicar general. The diocesan bishop can name any member of the Catholic faithful, a priest or a layperson, male or female, as the chancellor of his diocese.

For a person to be appointed chancellor of a diocese, he or she must be of good reputation, above suspicion, prudent, and have practical experience (c. 483). The primary functions of a chancellor include the secretariat duties of the diocesan curia, countersigning all the official documents of the diocesan bishop and vicar general, and being in charge of the diocesan archives (c. 484). In addition to the general archives, the chancellor is also in charge of the historical archives, the church archives, and the secret archives. The documents to be kept in the secret archives include: dispensations from occult matrimonial impediments granted in the internal forum, dispensations granted in the non-sacramental forum, a record of marriages celebrated in secret (c. 1133), precepts of admonition and rebuke imposed as a penal remedy (c. 1339 § 3), and criminal cases (penal processes, whether judicial or administrative in nature).

In order to safeguard the safety of the documents in the diocesan archives, canon 490 rules that only the diocesan bishop is to keep the key of the diocesan archive. He may, however, allow his chancellor to have a copy of the key in case of emergency or sudden death.

Is the diocesan bishop required by law to have a diocesan finance council and finance officer (financial administrator)?

Every diocesan bishop is required by law to have a finance council and finance officer to administer the diocesan finances (c. 492 § 1; c. 1280). Canon 492 paragraphs 2 and 3 spell out the qualifications needed to be named to the diocesan finance council. They are to be members of the Christian faithful who have expertise in finance and civil law and outstanding integrity. Persons "who are related to the diocesan bishop up to the fourth degree of consanguinity or affinity are excluded from the finance council" (c. 492 §3).

The primary functions of a diocesan finance council are to:

a. Advise the diocesan bishop and his financial administrator on financial policy and the investment of money and movable goods assigned to an endowment (c. 1305);
b. Advise the diocesan bishop on the appointment of a diocesan finance officer and his or her removal from office (c. 494 §§ 1-2);
c. Counsel the diocesan bishop before he imposes a moderate tax upon public juridical persons subject to his governance and an extraordinary and moderate tax upon other physical and juridical persons in his diocese (c. 1263);
d. Counsel the diocesan bishop before he embarks on more important acts of administration in light of the economic conditions of the diocese (c. 1277);
e. Advise the diocesan bishop in determining the acts of administration that go beyond the limits and manner of ordinary administration (c. 1281 § 2);
f. Advise the diocesan bishop in determining how to diminish the obligations of a will or a pious cause when their fulfillment becomes impossible because of diminished income or some other causes (c. 1310 § 2);
g. Counsel the diocesan bishop on the alienation of ecclesiastical goods (c. 1292); and
h. Counsel the diocesan bishop against any transaction that has the capacity to jeopardize the patrimonial condition of the diocese (c. 1295).

The diocesan bishop, after consulting his college of consultors and finance council, is to appoint a finance officer for a five-year term. The diocesan finance officer must be truly expert in financial affairs and renowned for honesty. He administers the ecclesiastical goods of the diocese under the authority of the bishop and renders an account of the receipts and expenditures at the end of each year to the diocesan finance council (c. 494).

The *1983 Code of Canon Law* is silent about whether a person who is related to the bishop up to the fourth degree of consanguinity or affinity can be named as a diocesan finance officer. However, one is of the view that practical prudence suggests that close relatives of the diocesan bishop are to be excluded from the office of diocesan financial administrator.

Is the diocesan bishop required by law to have consultative bodies to assist him in the pastoral governance of his diocese?

Because of the immense nature of the governance of a diocese, the law requires that different segments of the people of God in a diocese assist their diocesan bishop. The required consultative bodies are a presbyteral council and a college of consultors. The priests' council and the college of consultors are diocesan groupings composed of priests.

What is the diocesan presbyteral council?

Canon 495 § 1 makes the establishment of a presbyteral (or priests') council in every diocese obligatory when it declares that "in every diocese a presbyteral council is to be established, that is, a group of priests, which representing the presbyterate, is to be a senate of the bishop and which assists the bishop in the governance of the diocese according to the norms of law to promote as much as possible the pastoral good of the portion of the people of God entrusted to him."

Priests of a given diocese are to freely elect members from their group to form the priests' council. Priests who hold key positions, such as the office of the vicar general, episcopal vicar, or judicial vicar in the diocese are *ex officio* members of the diocesan priests' council, and the diocesan bishop is entitled to name other priests he deems suitable to be members of the priests' council. Canon 498 sets forth the criteria for membership on the diocesan priests' council. The qualifications are:

a. Any secular priest incardinated in the diocese;
b. Secular priests who are not incardinated; and
c. Priests who are members of some religious institutes or societies of apostolic life who reside in the diocese and exercise an office for the good of the diocese.

The diocesan bishop has the prerogative right to "convoke the presbyteral council, preside over it, and determine the questions to be treated by it or receive proposals from the members" (c. 500 § 1). The diocesan priests' council possesses "only a consultative vote. The diocesan bishop is to hear it in affairs of greater importance but needs its consent only in cases expressly defined by law" (c. 500 § 2). The presbyteral council cannot "act without the diocesan bishop, who alone has charge of making public those things which have been established according to the norm of paragraph 2 of canon 500."

What are the functions of the diocesan college of consultors?

Every diocesan bishop is required to have a college of consultors, whose members are to assist the diocesan bishop in his pastoral ministry of the diocese. The diocesan bishop freely appoints the members of the college of consultors from among the members of the presbyteral council. There should be between six and twelve members of the college of consultors. The members of the college of consultors are to be appointed for a five-year term, which may be renewed (c. 502 § 1). The diocesan bishop presides over the college of consultors.

The functions of the college of consultors include the following:

1. When a diocesan see has been vacant for a year, a diocesan administrator can grant excardination or incardination only with the consent of the college of consultors (c. 272);
2. Some members of the college are consulted by the papal legate on the selection of a diocesan bishop or a coadjutor bishop (c. 377 § 3);
3. The college is to elect a diocesan administrator within eight days of receiving notice of the death of the diocesan bishop (c. 421 § 1);
4. In the absence of an auxiliary bishop, the college of consultors is to inform the Apostolic See of the death of the diocesan bishop (c. 422);
5. Chancellors and other notaries cannot be removed from office by a diocesan administrator without the consent of the college of consultors (c. 485);
6. The diocesan bishop needs the consent of the college before embarking on acts of extraordinary administration (c. 1277); and

7. The diocesan bishop needs the consent of the college for the alienation of property beyond the amount specified by the conference of bishops (c. 1292 § 1).

Does the law require the establishment of a diocesan pastoral council in every diocese?

The establishment of a diocesan pastoral council is not mandatory, though it is highly recommended (c. 511). A diocesan pastoral council helps the diocesan bishop in investigating, considering, and proposing practical suggestions regarding those things that pertain to the pastoral works in the diocese. The members of a diocesan pastoral council are to be selected from among the "Christian faithful who are in full communion with the Catholic Church—clerics, members of institutes of consecrated life, and especially laity—who are designated in a manner determined by the diocesan bishop" (c. 5012 § 1). Like the priests' council, the diocesan pastoral council possesses only a consultative vote. The diocesan bishop presides over the deliberations of the diocesan pastoral council and he alone has the authority to make public the acts of the diocesan pastoral council.

What does the term "diocesan synod" mean?

A diocesan synod is "a group of selected priests and other members of the Christian faithful of a particular church who assist the diocesan bishop for the good of the whole diocesan community" (c. 460). A diocesan synod assists the diocesan bishop in discussing and formulating diocesan policies on matters pertaining to the life of his diocese. The goal of a diocesan synod is to help the diocesan bishop to enact particular laws and pastoral policies and to set goals and priorities for his diocese.

The 1997 document, *Instruction on Diocesan Synods*, issued jointly by the Congregation for the Bishops and the Congregation for the Evangelization of Peoples, mentions the following as the purposes of a diocesan synod:

- To assist the diocesan bishop in the exercise of the office proper to him, that of governing the Christian community;

- To promote acceptance of the Church's salvific doctrine and to encourage the faithful to follow Christ more faithfully;
- To foster the betterment of clerical life, the formation of the clergy, and the promotion of vocations to the priesthood and to religious life;
- To further evangelization, to review diocesan laws, policies, and guidelines, and, where necessary, to remedy lacunas to prevent abuses; and
- To evaluate pastoral programs and propose new pastoral plans where such are deemed necessary.

The diocesan bishop alone convokes a diocesan synod and presides over it either personally or through his delegate. He approves the agenda for the synod. According to canon 463, the following are can be invited to participate in a diocesan synod:

- A coadjutor bishop and auxiliary bishops;
- Vicars general, episcopal vicars, and judicial vicars;
- Members of the presbyteral council;
- Lay members of the Christian faithful, even members of institutes of consecrated life chosen by the pastoral council in a manner and number to be determined by the diocesan bishop;
- The rector of the diocesan major seminary and vicars forane;
- At least one priest from each vicariate forane chosen by all those who have care for souls there;
- Some superiors of religious institutes and societies of apostolic life that have a house in the diocese may be chosen. The diocesan bishop determines the number and how they are to be chosen; and
- The diocesan bishop may invite other members of the Christian faithful to participate in the synod. He may also invite other ministers of churches and ecclesial communities that are not in full communion with the Catholic Church as observers of the diocesan synod.

It is recommended that the diocesan bishop consults experts in canon law during the preparatory stages of the synod and when promulgating the synodal declarations. Synodal declarations could be acts of the *munus docendi* (that is, acts of faith and morals) or juridical in nature. Huels (2001) recommended that the juridical acts of a diocesan synod be promulgated as general administrative norms by means of the bishop's executive power. Diocesan synodal decrees are juridically invalid if they contradict the universal law of the Church, or the general decrees of particular councils or the conference of bishops *(The 1997 Instruction on Diocesan Synods)*.

The diocesan bishop is required by law to "communicate the text of the declarations and decrees of the synod to the Metropolitan and to the conference of bishops" (c. 467) to promote communion among bishops in the ecclesiastical province and in the entire country. The diocesan bishop disseminates the acts or results of the synod to all his priests in and outside of his diocese and to the religious houses, agencies, and institutions in his diocese. The *1997 Instruction on Diocesan Synods* requires the diocesan bishop to send, through the papal legate, a final copy of synodal decrees and declarations to the Congregation for Bishops or the Congregation for the Evangelization of Peoples, depending on whether the diocesan synod has taken place in mission or non-mission territories.

What happens when a diocese is impeded or becomes vacant?

The diocesan see is said to be impeded if the diocesan bishop is incapable of exercising his pastoral governance by reason "of captivity, banishment, exile, or incapacity" (c. 412). The diocesan see becomes vacant due to the death of a diocesan bishop or if the Bishop of Rome has accepted his resignation or transferred him (c. 416). In the interim, an administrator is to be elected to govern the diocese. The administrator is called "an apostolic administrator" if he is named by the Roman Pontiff. If the diocesan college of consultors elects him, he is called a diocesan administrator. Only a priest who has completed his thirty-fifth year of age can be named as an apostolic administrator or a diocesan administrator. An apostolic administrator or diocesan administrator is equivalent in law to a diocesan bishop. He, therefore, possesses the powers of pastoral governance and governs the diocese in his name once he is named as an apostolic administrator or is validly elected as a diocesan administrator by the college of consultors. However, his powers as an apostolic administrator or a diocesan administrator are limited. The Roman Pontiff always specifies the limits of the powers of an apostolic administrator in his letter of appointment.

A diocesan administrator cannot and should not perform any of the following acts: "approve diocesan association of the faithful" (c. 312 § 1 3°); "confer a canonry" in places where canonries exist in the cathedral or collegial churches (c. 509 § 1); or "remove the judicial vicar or adjutant judicial vicar" (c. 1420 § 5).

However, with the consent of the college of consultors, the diocesan administrator can validly "remove the chancellor and other notaries" (c. 485) and "issue dimissorial letters for ordination, but not to those who have been denied holy orders by the diocesan bishop" (c. 1018 § 2).

A diocesan administrator can also perform certain acts when the diocese has been vacant for a year. For instance, he can, with the consent of the college of consultors, grant excardination and incardination to a priest or priests and appoint pastors to parishes (c. 525, 2°).

Supra-diocesan Church Groupings

This section explores two groupings of particular churches: ecclesiastical provinces and bishops' conferences. The Second Vatican Council recommends the establishment of ecclesiastical provinces and episcopal conferences to promote and enhance common pastoral actions among different dioceses in a given province or a country.

What is an ecclesiastical province?

An ecclesiastical province is a grouping of dioceses, one of which must be an archdiocese with a metropolitan archbishop, while the others are suffragan dioceses. The archbishop only has a supervisory role in the governance of the suffragan dioceses. He must, however, report any abuses that may arise in the province to the Roman Pontiff. The archbishop presides over the meetings of the suffragan bishops and also of their ordinations. In his ecclesiastical province, a metropolitan archbishop has the authority to:

a. Exercise vigilance so that the faith and ecclesiastical discipline are observed carefully and inform the Roman Pontiff of abuses, if there are any;
b. Conduct a canonical visitation for a cause previously approved by the Apostolic See if a suffragan bishop has neglected it; and
c. Designate a diocesan administrator according to the norms of canons: 421 § 2, 425 § 3, 436 §§ 1-3).

A metropolitan archbishop and his suffragan bishops exercise their pastoral cooperation in a provincial council. An archbishop can convoke a provincial council only with the consent of the majority of the bishops in the province. The suffragan bishops must agree where a provincial council will be held, what the agenda will be, and who will be invited as guests. Metropolitan archbishops wear a pallium, the symbol of their communion with the Bishop of Rome, over their chasubles in solemn celebrations. The pallium is also a sign of their authority to supervise the pastoral governance of the suffragan dioceses under them.

Huels (2000) described a pallium as "a sort of woolen collar, with pendants back and front, and worn by the pope, by the patriarch of Jerusalem (though not a metropolitan), and metropolitan archbishops." New metropolitan archbishops are invited to the Vatican to receive their pallium on the feast day of Saints Peter and Paul on June 29 every year. A metropolitan archbishop can wear his pallium in every church in the ecclesiastical province under his supervision.

What are the primary functions and responsibilities of the bishops' conference?

The conference of bishops is "a form of assembly in which the bishops of a certain country or region exercise their pastoral office jointly in order to enhance the Church's beneficial influence on all men, especially by devising forms of the apostolate and apostolic methods suitably adapted to the circumstances of the times" (Flannery, 1998, p. 587).

An episcopal conference is a relatively new supra-diocesan structure in the Catholic Church. Two extraordinary synods of bishops (1965 and 1985) were called to study this new structure to safeguard the communion and collegiality of the Church. A brief exploration of the historical development of the episcopal conference will lead to a better understanding of the operation of this supra-diocesan structure.

Scholars often trace the origin of bishops' conferences as we have them today to Belgium, where, since political independence in 1830, the Archbishop of Malines (Mechelen) Most Rev. François Antoine De Man used to meet his suffragan bishops at his residence to discuss issues of common interest and to find solutions to common problems. Kutner (1972) pointed out that the first such meeting was held from November 16 to 19, 1830, and the bishops discussed some questions concerning liturgy, discipline, pastoral issues, and organization (p. 3). Kutner holds that the Belgian bishops often invited experts in various disciplines to counsel them on their deliberations on the issues affecting the local churches. The rector of the Catholic University of Louvain was occasionally invited to attend some of the sessions and occasionally civil officers were invited as well. The Belgian bishops' assembly adopted a set of statutes that spelled out the modalities of the "association" and how these meetings were to be conducted.

The German bishops started having their national meeting around 1848. Around this time, there was civil interference in some ecclesiastical affairs, such as the appointment of pastors and bishops. So the German bishops came together to address these challenges. At their Würzburg national assembly from October 22 to November 16, 1848, the bishops upheld "the right of the Church to educate youth, the Church's freedom and right to run her own affairs, no state interference in the Church's personnel appointment, the right of the Church to administer and to run her schools, and the right to teach religious doctrines in school and the right to establish and to run seminaries" (Kikoti, 1996, p. 17).

The National Conference of Catholic Bishops (NCCB) of the United States had a difficult time during its inception. It first began in 1918 as the "National Catholic War Council" (NCWC) to address issues arising from the country's involvement in the First World War. After the war, the American bishops realized the need to have an organization at the national level for consultation and the promotion of the Church's common interests. Cardinal James Gibbons, with the Apostolic See's backing, set up a committee to do a feasibility study on the possibility of the establishment of an organization at the national level. Pope Benedict XV approved the committee's proposal, and during their national assembly in September 1919, the bishops voted on the establishment of the National Catholic Welfare Council (NCWC) and elected its officers and administrative commission (Dulles, 1988, p. 528).

Some of the bishops had misgivings about this newly established organization and raised objections. So on February 25, 1922, Cardinal Cajeta de Lai, with the approval of Pope Pius XI, issued a decree of dissolution of the National Catholic Welfare Council. The reasons given for this move were these: "It was against canon law. It was expensive and had the tendency through Social Action Department to make controversial and divisive pronouncements. There was the likelihood that such a council would diminish the freedom of the individual diocesan bishops" (Dulles, 1988, p. 528).

Through the guidance of Bishop Schremb, the then diocesan bishop of Cleveland, the decree was later withdrawn. However, the National Council's initial authority was greatly weakened. It was forbidden to issue binding decrees and the word "council" had to be dropped from its title. After the Second Vatican Council, this national assembly of American bishops came to be known as the National Conference of Catholic Bishops (NCCB).

Realizing the valuable contribution of episcopal conferences, the Second Vatican Council declared:

> It is often impossible, nowadays especially, for bishops to exercise their office suitably and fruitfully unless they establish closer understanding and cooperation with other bishops. Since episcopal conferences—many such have already been established in different countries—have produced outstanding examples of a more fruitful apostolate, this sacred synod judges that it would be in the highest degree helpful if in all parts of the world, the bishops of each country or region would meet regularly, so that by sharing their wisdom and experience and exchanging views, they may jointly formulate a program for the common good of the Church (*CD*, 37).

The conciliar fathers went on to spell out who were to be the members of episcopal conferences, describe their juridical status, and recommend that the already existing conferences of bishops were to have statutes that were to be reviewed and approved by the Apostolic See. Thus, the conference of bishops assumed a new juridical character, as Feliciani (1988) put it:

> Conferences of bishops moved from unofficial meetings into instances framed by the Church's constitutional law, from voluntary assemblies into *coetus,* which were now obligatory in terms of both establishment and participation, from meetings which were heterogeneous in form and composition into essentially homogeneous *conventus,* from an organism of merely moral authority into institutions capable of making juridically binding deliberations, even if limited to specific matters and under rather rigorous conditions (p. 12).

Does a bishops' conference have any doctrinal authority?

The Second Vatican Council was very cautious not to create any intermediary organ between the supreme authority in the Church and the diocesan bishops. The Second Vatican Council never explicitly discussed the teaching authority of the conferences of bishops for fear that giving the conferences of bishops any doctrinal authority might lead to the regionalization of churches, which might diminish the autonomy and teaching authority of the individual bishops and eventually threaten the unity of the Church.

Conferences of bishops throughout the Latin Church have issued and continue to issue various types of documents, pastoral letters, and statements of a doctrinal nature, and yet canonists and theologians still debate whether the conferences of bishops have the power to teach authoritatively in the Church. Cardinal Joseph Ratzinger, now the retired Pope Benedict XVI, held that conferences of bishops as such do not have a *mandatum docendi.* To Ratzinger, this teaching office properly belongs to the pope, individual bishops, and the College of Bishops acting with its head, the pope. He declared that "no episcopal conference as such has a teaching mission; its documents have no authority of their own save that of the consent given to them by the individual bishops (Ratzinger, 1984, p. 60). Expressing a similar sentiment, Green (1987) declared that a conference of bishops in a given country or territory may exercise its teaching office, but it does not have the power to teach authoritatively, unless this power has been given to it by a special mandate from the Apostolic See. Similarly, Hamer and De Lubac held that the conference of bishops, which originated during the course of the historical experience of the Church, is of ecclesiastical origin and does not belong to the constitutive elements of the Church and as such does not have the *mandatum* to teach.

Notwithstanding the opinions advanced above, other scholars are of the view that conferences of bishops not only have pastoral and juridical relevance, but also a genuine theological foundation in the life of the Church. The theological foundation of the bishops' conference is rooted in the missionary nature of the Church. Conferences of bishops are of a great help in the Church's mission of evangelization, furthering the communion of the particular churches with the universal Church, thus facilitating the diocesan bishop's responsibility for the whole Church.

Dulles (1984) taught that the conferences of bishops exercise an authoritative task, which is essential to the very nature of the Church. He pointed out that these conferences are indirectly mandated by divine law to exercise this power, since it is the divine law that gives the hierarchy of the Church the insight and wisdom to establish this supra-diocesan structure, which is seen as very helpful and even necessary in the mission of the individual diocesan bishops. Dulles held that structures like parishes, dioceses, and the Roman Curia, as we have them in the Church today, are not constitutive elements of the Church. They were never willed by Christ, and yet they have real power and authority based on the divinely established structure of the Church. The conferences of bishops should be seen in the same light.

Urrutia (1989) declared, that "when the conference of bishops teaches, it teaches as such, and not the individual bishop insofar as they adhere to the opinions contained in the declaration. For this reason, religious submission (*obsequium religiosum*) is due to the opinions proposed by the conference both on the part of the bishops themselves and on the part of the faithful of their churches" (p. 209). Supporting the views expressed by Urrutia, Manzanares asserted that "the episcopal conference legitimately established as a unity and acting according to its statutes is capable of exercising an authoritative magisterium and is juridically empowered to exercise this *de facto*" (p. 263).

When one critically examines the conciliar pronouncement on the conferences of bishops in *Christus Dominus* numbers 37 and 38, one sees some traces of doctrinal authority being attributed to the conferences of bishops. The Second Vatican Council describes the bishops' conference as an assembly through which bishops of a given country or certain territory jointly exercise their pastoral office. The pastoral office, *munus pastorale,* of bishops, as explained in article 11 of the same document, includes the threefold *munera* of Christ: teaching, sanctifying, and governing. Thus, *munus pastorale,* as used in *Christus Dominus* number 38, includes teaching authority as well. Based on this understanding, one may conclude that the bishops' conference, as an organ of the Church at the supra-diocesan level, has the power to teach authoritatively in the Church.

What are the internal structures of a bishops' conference?

An episcopal conference is a public juridical person (c. 451). As a juridical public person, each conference of bishops is to have its proper statutes, which have to receive *recognitio* from the Apostolic See. Each conference of bishops is to have a "permanent committee of bishops and a general secretariat" (c. 451); a president, a vice president, a secretary general, and other officers are to be elected to perform certain functions for the conference (c. 452). Canon 457 requires every conference of bishops to have a permanent council or committee, which prepares an agenda for the plenary meetings and is charged with the responsibility of implementing the acts and decrees of the plenary meetings.

The primary functions of the secretariat of episcopal conferences are to:

1. Prepare a report of the acts and decrees of a conference's plenary meeting and the acts of the permanent council of bishops, communicate the same to all the members of the conference, and draw up other acts whose preparation the

president of the conference or the council entrusts to the general secretary; and

2. Communicate to the neighboring conferences of bishops the acts and documents that the conference in the plenary meeting or the permanent council of bishops decides to send to them. (c. 458)

Conferences of bishops are encouraged to foster and promote a good working relationship with neighboring conferences to serve the greater good of the universal Church. Conferences of bishops are to inform the Apostolic See of all their actions and programs that have global reach (c. 459).

CHAPTER 4

The Parish Church

What is a parish church?

The universal law of the Church rules that every diocese or an ecclesiastical grouping equivalent in law to a diocese be divided into distinct parts called parishes. Thus, a parish is a community of Catholic Christians stably established within a particular church, whose pastoral care is entrusted to its proper pastor under the authority of the diocesan bishop (c. 515 § 1). According to Arrieta (2000), a parish church "represents a part of the diocese entrusted to the diocesan bishop with the pastor as his cooperator in the care of souls" (p. 247).

The parish church constitutes a community of faith, where the members of the Catholic Church learn, experience, and practice their Catholic faith. Pope John Paul II described the parish church as a home where the members of the body of Christ gather together, are open to meeting God the Father and the Savior Jesus Christ, are incorporated into the Church by the Holy Spirit by virtue of their baptism, and are ready to accept each other as brothers and sisters with fraternal love, regardless of their condition, race, and origin. Commenting on the functions of a parish church, Pope John Paul II declared that a parish church is to "provide the Church's great service to the members of the mystical body of Christ by praying in common, reading, and meditating on the Word of God, celebrating the sacraments, most especially the Eucharist, embarking on catechesis for the young people and adult faith formation" (February 5, 1997).

A parish church may be territorial or personal. It is territorial when it "embraces all Christ's faithful of a given territory" (c. 518).

The Catholic Christians living within the circumscriptions of that given territory will be members of the parish church established to serve the people in that geographical area. The parish church may be a personal parish when it is "established by reason of the rite, language, or nationality of Christ's faithful of a certain territory or even for some other reason" (c. 518). Canon 813 recommends the establishment of a parish for university students to serve the pastoral and spiritual needs of the students, the faculty, and the other constituents of the university. Thus, a parish erected for a university in response to this recommendation is a personal parish church. A parish established to serve the pastoral and spiritual needs of military personnel would be a personal parish church. Another example of a personal parish is a parish for people of Italian or Ghanaian descent living within a certain territory.

Does the law require every parish to have its proper pastor?

Every parish is to have its proper parish priest or pastor, who governs the parish in his own name but under the authority of the diocesan bishop. The parish priest "is the proper pastor of the parish entrusted to him under the authority of the diocesan bishop, whose ministry of Christ he is called to share, so that for this community, he may carry out the offices of teaching, sanctifying, and ruling with the cooperation of other priests or deacons and with the assistance of lay members of Christ's faithful, in accordance with the law" (c. 519). Thus, a parish priest or a pastor is a constitutive element of a parish church. There cannot be a parish without its proper pastor or parish priest. A parish that is validly erected enjoys juridical personality by law (c. 515 § 3) and is represented by the parish priest, who acts "in the person of the parish" (c. 532).

For validity, a pastor of a parish church must be a priest or a bishop. This means a deacon or a layperson cannot be validly named to the office of pastor. For liceity or lawfulness, in order to be appointed to the office of pastor, a priest must be outstanding in sound doctrine and integrity, endowed with a zeal for souls and other virtues, such as prudence in judgment, and must possess the necessary human skills to deal with people effectively.

The law requires that pastors have some permanence in office, and therefore, they must be appointed for an indefinite period or for some specific time. The determination of how long a pastor is to be appointed is left to the conferences of bishops to decide. The common practice in the United States is that a diocesan bishop often appoints pastors for a six-year term. The possibility of renewing this term is left to the discretion of each diocesan bishop. It is common in Europe to be a pastor to a parish for eight years or for life.

What are the principal functions of a parish priest or a pastor?

Canon 530 of the *1983 Code of Canon Law* mentions the following as the principal functions of a parish priest:

1. The administration of baptism;
2. The administration of the sacrament of confirmation to those who are in danger of death, according to the norms of canon 883 no. 3;
3. The administration of viaticum and of the anointing of the sick, without prejudice to the prescript of canon 1003 § 2, and the imparting of the apostolic blessing;
4. Assistance at marriages and the nuptial blessing;
5. The performance of funeral rites;
6. The blessing of the baptismal font at Easter time, the leading of processions outside the church, and giving solemn blessings outside the church; and
7. The performance of the more solemn Eucharistic celebration on Sundays and holy days of obligation.

When does the office of a parish priest or a pastor cease?

The office of a pastor ceases in one of the following ways: removal, transfer, resignation, or the end of the term. A parish priest who is appointed for a specific term can only be removed from office for a grave reason. A parish priest can be removed from office because of one of the following reasons:

a. Bringing grave harm to the ecclesiastical community;

b. Permanent illness of mind or body rendering him incapable of pastoral ministry;
c. Loss of a good reputation among the upright and responsible parishioners;
d. A grave neglect of official duties or a violation of parochial duties which persists after a series of warnings; and
e. Poor administration of the temporal goods of the church.

A diocesan bishop may transfer a parish priest for any just reason. If the parish priest is unwilling to leave his parish, the diocesan bishop is to observe the norms of transfer as stipulated in canons 1400 to 1403. Parish priests are required by the universal law of the Church to resign at the age of seventy-five. They may resign at an earlier age for health reasons, and the diocesan bishop must accept their resignation. The office of a parish priest ceases when the term of his appointment ends and he is notified of it.

Who is a parochial vicar or associate pastor?

A parochial vicar or associate pastor is a priest appointed by a diocesan bishop to assist a parish priest or a pastor in the pastoral ministry of his parish. A diocesan bishop may appoint one or more parochial vicars (associate pastors) to help a parish priest of a given parish if the pastoral needs of the parish demand more than the services of one priest. According to Bachofen (1926), the office of a parochial vicar "grew out of the various degrees of the minor offices in the Church" (p. 236). Though a parochial vicar shares in the ministry of teaching, sanctifying, and governance of the parish, he needs the pastor's permission to celebrate baptism, confirmation, anointing of the sick, and assisting at marriages in the parish. The pastor and his assistant(s) are not working *in solidum* and do not possess equal powers and faculties. The parochial vicar is accountable to the pastor, and he exercises his priestly ministry in the parish under the authority of the parish priest. As a co-worker with the pastor and sharing in his solicitude, the pastor is to discuss his pastoral plans with his assistant so as to promote cooperation and effective parish ministry. Describing a parochial vicar as a co-worker or cooperator, canon 545 § 1 presupposes an ongoing consultation so that a parochial vicar can have access to relevance to enhance his ministry.

Is there any relationship between a parish church and a diocesan bishop?

The parish church does not exist in a vacuum, advancing its own purpose and agenda. It exists among other parishes within a given diocese. It has a theological bond with these other parishes, the diocese, and with the universal Church through the diocesan bishop. This theological bond informs and directs its relationship with the other parishes, the diocese, and the whole Church. Coriden (1997) identified the five types of relationships in the parish church. He mentioned its relationship with the diocese, with nearby Catholic parishes, with more distant Catholic parishes, with the local Protestant, Jewish, and other religious communities, and with civil society (p. 101).

The parish is thus linked to the universal Church through the theological bond it has with the diocese of which it is a part. The diocesan bishop is the visible and unifying link between a parish church and the other parishes in his diocese and at the same time the link between the parish church and the universal Church. It is, therefore, crucial that parishioners are reminded at every Eucharistic celebration that they are "a part of something larger than (themselves), something called the communion of saints. The parish church at worship is connected historically with the apostles, martyrs, and the saints of old. It is connected with other worshiping communities around the world. And it is connected in communion with the local churches that make up the diocese under the leadership of the (diocesan) bishop" (Coriden, 1997, p. 103). At every Eucharistic celebration, the names of the pope and the diocesan bishop are mentioned and prayed for, because the pope and the diocesan bishop are the visible signs of the parish church's participation in the communion of the universal Church as well as in the diocesan church.

The nearby Catholic parishes are grouped into what are called deaneries or vicariates under the leadership of a vicar. It is recommended that the local pastors in a given deanery or vicariate meet regularly to share pastoral experiences, encourage each other, exchange information regarding their parish ministry, and strategize common pastoral planning to embark on a common pastoral activity and promote effective parish ministries and administration. Such regular meetings among neighboring pastors promote and fuel active relationships among neighboring parishes.

Some parishes may enter into a partnership with other parishes in different parts of their diocese or parishes on different continents to share common resources and to promote effective evangelization. Such partnership promotes solidarity and Christian love among parishes in the Catholic communion.

Canon 755 § 1 of the *1983 Code of Canon Law* recommends the active participation of parish churches in ecumenical dialogue with local Protestant ecclesial communities to restore "unity among all Christians, which by the will of Christ, the Church is bound to promote." Catholic parishes are encouraged to join other Christian ecclesial communities in praying for Christian unity and promoting mutual respect among the followers of Christ. On the parish church's relationship with civil society, canon 225 § 2 declares that parishioners of a given parish are "bound by a particular duty to imbue and perfect the order of the temporal affairs with the spirit of the Gospel and thus to witness to Christ, especially in carrying out these same affairs and in exercising secular functions." It is in the light of this understanding that Coriden (1997) asserted that social action and community development are to be part of the parish's agenda, because "the parish community should be engaged with the social problems around it. It should be a part of efforts to promote social justice, to eliminate racial and ethnic discrimination, to combat crime and drug abuse, to encourage housing for the poor and elderly, to improve public education, to curb violence and develop alternative dispute resolution, and to stabilize employment and opportunities" (p. 107).

What are the principal functions of a parish church?

Speaking on the primary purpose of a parish church, Pope John Paul II declared that a parish church is:

> To provide the Church's great services: prayer in common, and the reading of God's Word, celebrations of the

sacraments, especially that of the Eucharist, catechesis for
children and adult catechumenate, the ongoing formation of
the faithful, communications designed to make the Christian
message known, services of charity and solidarity, and the
local work of movement (February 5, 1997).

Based on the above statement, the primary duties of a parish
church can be grouped into the following four categories:

A. Proclamation of the Gospel message and faith formation. Here
   emphasis is to be placed on:

   a. Preaching the Word of God (cc. 762; 767; 771);
   b. Forming the members of the parish community in the
      tradition of the Church and helping them to grow in their
      faith and Christian living (cc. 777; 779);
   c. Embarking on catechetical instruction and programs to
      cultivate, nurture, and sustain the Catholic faith in the
      parish community (cc. 775 and 776); and
   d. Promoting sacramental instruction and Catholic education
      (cc. 851; 794; 796; 798).

B. Worship and Sacramental celebrations.
   Parishioners are to be encouraged to participate actively in the
   celebrations of the Sunday liturgy (cc. 897; 899) and to receive
   the other sacraments.

C. Embarking on works of charity and care by:
   a. Taking care of orphans and widows; and
   b. Providing shelter for the homeless, feeding the hungry, and
      helping to settle new immigrants.

D. Having outreach and social action programs as a means of:
   a. Evangelizing and winning more souls for Christ (cc. 771 §
      2; 781; 791) and
   b. Preaching and promoting social justice (cc. 222 § 2; 768
      § 2).

Are there any required ecclesial bodies at the parish level to assist in parish administration?

The *1983 Code of Canon Law* mentions the establishment of two parochial councils to assist pastors or parish priests in parish administration. While the establishment of a parish finance council is mandatory (c. 537), a parish pastoral council is optional (c. 536).

What are the primary functions of a parish finance council?

Canon 537 makes the establishment of a parish finance council mandatory by declaring that "in each parish, there is to be a finance council, which is governed, in addition to the universal law, by norms issued by the diocesan bishop and in which the Christian faithful, selected according to these same norms, are to assist the pastor in the administration of the goods of the parish without prejudice to the prescript of canon 532." Thus, the parish finance council is to assist the parish priest in financial matters and in the general administration of the parish. Members of a parish finance council are to be truly skillful in financial affairs or civil law, and they are to give their parish priest an informed counsel on financial policy and investment.

The parish pastoral council: How does it assist in the pastoral ministry of a parish?

Although the establishment of a parish pastoral council is optional, a diocesan bishop may decree the establishment of a parish pastoral council in every parish in his diocese. A parish pastoral council, like a diocesan pastoral council, possesses only a consultative vote and is governed by the norms established by the diocesan bishop. Members of a parish pastoral council may be selected or appointed from the various segments of the parish and are to help their pastor in drawing pastoral plans for the parish and advising him on pastoral initiatives and activities for the parish.

CHAPTER 5

The Teaching and Sanctifying Offices of the Church

This chapter explores the principal functions of the Church: teaching and sanctifying. On the teaching ministry, it examines the source of the Church's authority to teach doctrine and morals; who the authentic teachers of the faith are; and what are the means through which doctrines and morals are communicated to Catholic Christians. The sanctifying ministry focuses on the seven sacraments and their celebration and significance in the life of a Catholic Christian. As an important component of the sanctifying office, the author explores how the Church promotes healing and fairness to its members who feel alienated from the Church or who have been unjustly treated by the officials of the Church.

Teaching office of the church: Does the Catholic Church have any authority to teach doctrine and morals?

From its inception, the Catholic Church has viewed teaching as central to its purpose and mission. After the Resurrection, Jesus Christ gave a mandate to his early followers to teach all nations and to make all people his disciples when he declared: "Go, therefore, and make disciples of all nations, baptizing them in the name of the Father, and of the Son, and of the Holy Spirit, teaching them to observe all that I have commanded you" (Mt 28: 19-20). By these words, Jesus Christ entrusted the deposit of faith to the Church. The Church receives its authority to teach doctrine and morals from its founder Jesus Christ. The Church, with the assistance of the Holy Spirit, protects the deposit of faith it received from its founder with reverence, examines it ever more closely, and proclaims and expounds it faithfully. Thus, the Church has a divine duty and right to teach the doctrine it received to all people. It is in the light of this insight that the Church always and everywhere teaches "moral principles, even about the social order, and to render affairs insofar as the fundamental rights of the human person or the salvation of souls requires it" (c. 747 § 2).

It is true that the Church's mission is a religious one, and not a political, economic, or social one. It is equally true that the religious function of the Church can contribute to the building of a vibrant society and strengthening of the human community. Thus, the teaching of moral principles on social and economic issues is critical in the development of the human person. In its attempts to continue to spread justice and charity within countries and among international communities, the Church makes a moral judgment whenever it sees any abuse of basic human rights or sees the salvation of souls being threatened.

Though the Church encourages Catholic Christians to participate in this "prophetic function" of teaching as Jesus Christ commanded his followers to do, participation in the teaching ministry of the Church varies depending on one's grade or standing. The apostles entrusted the teaching office to the College of Bishops, who shared the teaching ministry with the priests who worked closely with them.

The Church's mission to teach the whole world can be categorized as the ministry of the divine Word (which includes preaching and catechesis), missionary activity, Catholic education in schools, universities, and ecclesiastical universities, and the media (Beal et al., 2000).

What is the ecclesiastical magisterium of the Church?

The magisterium is the teaching office of the church. It is the official teaching office charged with interpreting and expounding the word of God authentically under the authority and in the name of Jesus Christ. This office consists of the Roman Pontiff and the College of Bishops, because the task of interpreting the Word of God authentically has been entrusted solely to the pope and to the bishops in communion with him. In Matthew 28:19-20, Jesus Christ first entrusted the ministry of teaching and interpreting the word authentically to the apostles. The apostles then transmitted the ministry of teaching the Word of God to their successors: the pope and the College of Bishops.

The task of giving an authentic interpretation of the Word of God, whether in its written form or in the form of tradition, has been entrusted to the living teaching office of the Church alone. The teaching office exercises its teaching authority in the name of Jesus. The magisterium is a servant to the Word of God, and not superior to it, and so it teaches only what has been handed down to it since its beginning. What this office proposes for belief is carefully and divinely "drawn from the single deposit of faith" (*DV*, 10). In this exercise, the magisterium listens carefully to the divine Word, "guards it with dedication, and expounds it faithfully" (*DV*, 10). It is in the light of this insight and understanding that the Church teaches that the magisterium is infallible in exercising its teaching authority.

The infallibility of the magisterium means that when the magisterium defines a solemn doctrine regarding faith and morals, the Holy Spirit guides it, and therefore, it cannot err. The doctrine of the infallibility of the magisterium is deeply rooted in the history of the Church. This doctrine was solemnly articulated in the final session of the First Vatican Council. The biblical foundation of the doctrine of infallibility is found in Jesus's promise to send the Holy Spirit to guide the apostles to all truth (Jn 16:12-14). Infallible teaching is exercised by the Roman Pontiff when he speaks *ex cathedra,* that is, when as Supreme Pastor and teacher of all the Catholic faithful, he "proclaims by definitive act that a doctrine of faith or morals is to be held" (c. 749 § 1). Though the Holy Father has the privilege of infallibility, he rarely uses it. His teachings by means of encyclicals, exhortations, letters, addresses, and homilies are not infallible.

Individual bishops do not enjoy the privilege of infallibility. However, they do teach infallibly on the following condition:

> When, even though dispersed throughout the world, but preserving for all that among themselves and with Peter's successor the bond of communion, in their authoritative teaching concerning matters of faith and morals, they are in agreement that a particular teaching is to be held

definitively and absolutely. This is still more clearly the case,
when, assembled in an ecumenical council, they are for the
universal Church, teachers of and judges in matters of faith
and morals, whose decisions must be adhered to with loyal
and obedient assent of faith (*LG*, 25).

Catholic Christians are bound by the authentic teaching of the
magisterium. They are to adhere to the doctrines declared definitively
with the loyal and obedient assent of faith.

If all Catholic Christians are encouraged to participate in the "prophetic mission" of the Church, why does the Church limit the ministry of preaching to the ordained?

All Catholic Christians participate in the evangelizing mission of
the Church by virtue of their baptism and confirmation. The Church
teaches that there is "diversity of ministry, but unity of mission" (*AA*,
2) in participating in the work of Christ.

Preaching is an authoritative proclamation of the doctrine of the
Church. In the early Christian gatherings, as recorded in the Acts of
the Apostles, the early believers always gathered together to listen
to the preaching of Peter (Acts 2: 22-42) and the other apostles
(Acts 13: 16-41).

Thus, the above-mentioned question should be tackled in two
ways:

- The Christian faithful who must preach:
  o The bishops "have the right to preach the Word of God
    everywhere, including churches and oratories of religious
    institutes of pontifical right, unless the local bishop has
    expressly forbidden it in particular cases" (c. 763). Thus,
    bishops can preach in any part of the church.
- The Christian faithful who can preach:
  o Priests and deacons can only preach the Word of God
    when they are given the faculties to do so in churches
    within their own diocese and other dioceses. The laity may
    be permitted to preach the Word of God in churches "if
    necessity requires it in certain circumstances or if it seems

> advantageous in particular cases, according to the prescripts
> of the conference of bishops and without prejudice to canon
> 767 § 1." (c. 766).

One can conclude from the above that the lay faithful can participate in the ministry of preaching in certain particular cases.

Preaching a homily is an exclusive right of the clergy, because a homily is an integral part of the celebration of the sacred liturgy, and thus it is fitting that it is reserved to those who lead the celebration. In giving a homily, one must explain the mysteries of faith and the norms of Christian life using the sacred text as a point of reference (c. 767 § 1).

Laypeople are on the forefront of the other forms of proclaiming the Catholic doctrines and transmitting the faith to others (catechesis, mission work, and Catholic education). The lay faithful are very active in the systematic teaching of Catholic doctrine and life in an attempt "to develop in men a living, explicit, and active faith" (*CD*, 14). Responding to the mandate of Jesus to proclaim his Gospel to all nations, the Church sends out missionaries, both clergy and lay faithful, to every corner of the globe to proclaim the Gospel and to baptize. Catholic educators participate in the evangelizing mission of the Church by sharing in her the teaching office of the Church, because Catholic educators "have the duty or privilege to ensure that students receive instructions in Catholic doctrine and practices. This requires that a public witness to the way of Christ, as found in the Gospel and upheld by the church's magisterium, shapes all aspects of an institution's life, both inside and outside the classroom. Divergence from this vision weakens Catholic identity and, far from advancing freedom, inevitably leads to confusion, whether moral, intellectual, or spiritual" (Pope Benedict XVI, April 17, 2008).

Laypeople who teach theology in Catholic universities or Catholic institutes of higher learning participate in the teaching office of the Church, and therefore, there should be a relationship between bishops and theologians. Thus the Church requires that "those who teach theological disciplines in any Catholic institutes of higher studies whatsoever must have a mandate from the competent ecclesiastical authority" (c. 812). The giving of the mandate to teach theological disciplines in the name of the Church is meant to uphold the orthodoxy of the Church's teaching and to ensure that teachers are in full communion with the Church.

Sanctifying office of the Church: Who instituted the seven sacraments and what is their significance?

The Catholic Church believes and teaches that there are seven sacraments and that Christ himself instituted these sacraments; therefore, they have divine origin. The sacraments are: baptism, confirmation, the Eucharist, penance, the anointing of the sick, holy orders, and matrimony. The seven sacraments touch all stages and important moments of Christian life: They bring about rebirth and an increase in the family of Jesus, healing and enhancing the mission of the Christian life of faith. The sacraments of baptism, confirmation, and the Eucharist lay the foundation of a Christian life. The seven sacraments can be grouped under two main categories: non-repeatable sacraments and repeatable sacraments.

What are the non-repeatable sacraments?

The sacraments of baptism, confirmation, and holy orders can be received only once. Anyone who is validly baptized cannot be baptized again. The same truth holds for those who have been validly confirmed or ordained. The reason is that upon the reception of each one of these sacraments, an indelible character or mark is imprinted on the soul of the recipient (c. 845 § 1) and therefore, the recipient cannot receive the sacrament again.

What are the repeatable sacraments?

The repeatable sacraments are the Eucharist, penance, the anointing of the sick, and marriage. However, a marriage validly celebrated cannot be repeated until one of the parties dies. These sacraments do not imprint any indelible character on the soul of the recipient, and therefore, can be received more than once in one's lifetime.

What is the sacrament of baptism?

Through the sacrament of baptism, we become members of the Catholic Church and are, thus, incorporated into Christ's Church and constituted persons in it with the duties and rights proper to a Christian lifestyle. When validly conferred by true water and the proper form of words, the sacrament of baptism frees us from sin and we are configured to Christ by an indelible character and thus become sons and daughters of our Father in heaven. The sacrament of baptism is a gateway to the other sacraments, because one who is baptized can validly receive the other sacraments (c. 842 § 1).

Who can receive baptism in the Church?

The church teaches that "every person not yet baptized and only such a person is able to be baptized" (c. 864).

Under what conditions can one be baptized in the Church?

As a sacrament of faith, baptism can only be conferred when one exhibits some level of faith within the community of believers with the exception of infant baptism. The faith that is required for baptism need not be "perfect" or "mature faith," but an incipient faith. It is in the light of this understanding that, before receiving baptism, one's godparent is asked, "What do you ask of God's Church?" The response is, "Faith."

Since infants lack the capacity to make a personal profession of faith in the Lord Jesus, their parents and those who act as godparents make this profession of faith on behalf of the child who is to be baptized. Before making this profession of faith, the parents and godparents are to be properly instructed in the meaning of the sacrament of baptism, their responsibility in forming the child in the practice of the faith, and their obligations as parents and godparents. It is in the light of all this that canon 851 declares:

> The parents of a child who is to be baptized, and those who
> are to undertake the function of sponsor are to be instructed
> properly on the meaning of the sacrament and the obligations

attached to it. The pastor personally or through others is to take care that the parents are properly instructed through both pastoral advice and common prayer, bringing several families together and where possible, visiting them.

The godparents are not only required to be physically present at the time of baptism, but more importantly, they are required to help and to guide their godchild to lead a holy Christian life in accordance with his or her baptismal promises (c. 872).

Who can play the role of a godparent?

To be permitted to play the role of godparent or a sponsor, one must be:

- Appointed by the candidate for baptism or by the parent. The person must be suitable and freely accept being a sponsor;
- Not less than sixteen years of age, unless the diocesan policies suggest otherwise;
- A Catholic who has been confirmed and has received the blessed Eucharist and leads a life of faith that befits the role to be undertaken;
- Not bound by any canonical penalty that was legitimately imposed or declared; and
- Not the father or mother of the person to be baptized (874, nos. 1-5).

In a situation where it is difficult to find a Catholic Christian to undertake the role of a godparent or sponsor, a non-Catholic member of an ecclesial community may be admitted to undertake the role of a witness (c. 874 §2).

Who can baptize in the name of the Church?

The ordinary minister of baptism is a bishop, a priest, or in the Latin Church, a deacon (c. 861 § 1). When the ordinary minister is absent or impeded, a lawful layperson can be designated to baptize, or if the supplicant is in danger of death, any person with the right intention, that is, the intention of the Church, can confer baptism lawfully and validly (c. 861 § 2). In the case of necessity or in danger of death, any person, even someone who is not baptized, can baptize, provided he or she has the required intention to do what the Church does when baptizing and to use the Trinitarian form of the baptismal formula.

Notwithstanding the provision of canon 861 § 1 for cases in danger of death, the administration of baptism is a parochial function. Thus, a believer is to be baptized in his or her parish church by his or her proper pastor or his delegate. It is unlawful for anyone to confer baptism outside his own territory without due permission, except in cases of the danger of death or other necessities (c. 862). The canon thus reminds pastors that they cannot validly baptize anyone, even their own subjects, outside their own territory unless they have received the required permission or except in cases of the danger of death.

What are the effects of the sacrament of baptism?

The sacrament of baptism produces the following effects:

- It forgives sins, original sin as well as personal sins (*CCC*, 1263);
- It makes us "new creatures," adopted sons and daughters of God (*CCC*, 1265);
- It impacts sanctifying grace, enabling the baptized to believe in God, to hope, and to act under the prompting of the Holy Spirit through the gifts of the Holy Spirit (*CCC*, 1266);
- It makes the baptized into members of the body of Christ and members of one another (*CCC*, 1267); and
- It constitutes the foundation of communion among all Christians, even including those who are not in full communion with the Catholic Church (*CCC*, 1271).

Why do we need the sacrament of confirmation if we have already received the Holy Spirit in baptism?

Though we do receive the Holy Spirit and thus become children of God in baptism, we still need the sacrament of confirmation because it "strengthens the baptized and obliges them more firmly to be witnesses of Christ by word and deed and to spread and defend the faith. It imprints a character, enriches by the gift of the Holy Spirit the baptized continuing on the path of Christian initiation, and binds them more perfectly to the Church" (c. 879). In the Latin Church, the sacrament of confirmation completes our initiation into the mystery of Christ. Confirmation is called "chrismation" because it is conferred by means of anointing with the oil of chrism on the forehead.

Who can be confirmed in the Church?

Any baptized Catholic Christian who has not been confirmed is capable of receiving this sacrament (c. 889 § 1). The sacrament of confirmation is to be conferred on candidates when they reach the age of reason. The question regarding the appropriate age to receive the sacrament is left to various conferences of bishops to decide for their respective territories. A baptized non-Catholic Christian of the ecclesial community who wishes to be received to full communion with the Catholic Church is admitted through a rite of reception, which is to take place during a liturgical celebration.

Who is the ordinary minister of the sacrament of confirmation?

The ordinary minister of confirmation in the Latin Church is a bishop. A priest may validly confer the sacrament of confirmation "if he has the faculty to do so, either from the universal law or by way of a special grant from competent authority" (c. 882). In the Eastern Catholic Churches, the ordinary minister of confirmation or chrismation is a bishop or a priest.

For validity, the celebration of the sacrament must follow the proper prescribed matter and form. The prescribed matter is anointing the forehead of the recipient with the oil of chrism. The oil must be consecrated by a bishop, even if a priest administers the sacrament (c. 880). The imposition of hands is the essence of the sacrament, and this is done when the minister faces the people and invites them to pray silently. Then the minister and the concelebrants extend their hands over the candidates (this implies laying hands on them) and the minister says the consecratory prayer. In the Latin Church, the prescribed form of confirmation is: "Be sealed with the Holy Spirit." The matter (that is, the anointing with oil of chrism on the forehead of the candidate) and the form (that is, "Be sealed with the Holy Spirit") are done simultaneously.

What is the sacrament of holy orders?

The sacrament of holy orders is instituted by Christ in which some members of the Christian faithful are identified as sacred ministers of the Church. These sacred ministers have been "consecrated and designated, each according to his grade, to nourish the people of God, fulfilling in the person of Christ the head the functions of teaching, sanctifying, and governing" (c. 1008). The sacrament of holy orders is divided into three grades: the order of deacons, the order of priesthood, and the order of bishops. To be admitted into holy orders, one must be a male baptized Catholic who has freely asked to be ordained (c. 1026). The sacrament of holy orders is conferred by "the laying on of hands and the prayer of consecration which the liturgical books prescribe for each grade. The ordinary minister of holy orders is a bishop" (c. 1012).

There are two types of deacons: transitional deacons and permanent deacons. The transitional deacons move onto the priesthood, while the permanent diaconate is a terminating order. The required age for admission into the holy order is contingent upon the grade at which one will be ordained.

A transitional deacon must be at least twenty-three years of age at the time of his ordination, while a permanent deacon must be at least thirty-five and must be ordained with the expressed consent of his wife. A candidate for the priesthood must be at least twenty-five (c. 1031 § 1). The bishops' conference of a given country or territory may establish a higher age for candidates for the priesthood and permanent diaconate depending on the special circumstances of their country or territory (c. 1031 § 3). Canon 1037 requires candidates who are unmarried and about to be admitted into the permanent diaconate and those who are to be admitted to the transitional diaconate, on the way to the priesthood, to undertake in a prescribed rite, publicly before God and the Church, the obligation of celibacy, unless they have taken perpetual vows in a religious institute.

Are there any impediments that can prevent someone from receiving holy orders?

A candidate who is bound by an impediment cannot be admitted to holy orders. Such an impediment may be simple, perpetual, or an irregularity. A simple impediment is not permanent: for instance, a marriage is a simple impediment that prevents one from being ordained into the priesthood. However, if one's wife dies, the impediment no longer exists, and one is free to be admitted to the priesthood if one wishes to become a priest. Canon 1042 mentions the following as simple impediments that bar one from being admitted to priesthood:

- A man who has a wife;
- A man who exercises an office or administration forbidden to clerics in accordance with the norms of canons 285 and 286 for which he must render an account, until he becomes free by having relinquished the office or administration and rendered the account; and
- A neophyte, unless he has been proven sufficiently in the judgment of the ordinary.

Perpetual impediments or irregularities are permanent in nature. These irregularities include any form of insanity, any form of psychological infirmity, and any offense of apostasy, heresy, or schism. A person who has committed a willful homicide, who has procured an abortion or attempted suicide, or who has gravely mutilated himself or another cannot be admitted to holy orders (c. 1041). Before a person is admitted to the holy orders, he must prove beyond any doubt that he has no traces of any of these infirmities or crimes and has completed the required studies in philosophy, theology, and other related disciplines.

Canon 1045 maintains that ignorance of these impediments does not exempt one from them. The law recommends that an ordination be celebrated during Mass at the cathedral. For pastoral reasons, it may be celebrated at a parish church (c. 1011).

What is the proper form and matter for a valid ordination?

The required matter and form for a valid ordination are the laying on of hands by the officiating minister or ministers and the consecratory prayer, which the liturgical books prescribe for individual grades. The laying on of hands by the officiating bishop (and of the concelebrating priests, in case of priestly ordination) must be done in silence.

The prescribed form of ordination is the consecratory prayer the bishop pronounces during the ordinations of a bishop, priest, or deacon. The proper form for ordaining bishops reads "So now pour out upon this chosen one that power which is from you, the governing Spirit whom you give to your beloved Son, Jesus Christ, the Spirit given by him to the holy apostles, who founded the Church in every place to be your temple for the unceasing glory and praise of your name."

The proper form for ordaining priests reads: "Almighty Father, grant to these servants of yours the dignity of the priesthood. Renew within them the Spirit of holiness. As co-workers with the order of bishops, may they be faithful to the ministry that they receive from you, Lord God, and be to each other a model of right conduct."

The form for deacons reads: "Lord, send forth upon them the Holy Spirit, that they may be strengthened by the gift of your sevenfold grace to carry out faithfully the work of the ministry" (Huels, 2009; cf. *Pontificalis Romani recognitio,* June 18, 1968).

Why does the Church hold the sacrament of the Eucharist in high honor?

The sacrifice of the Eucharist is held in high esteem among all the sacraments because it is through the holy Eucharist that Christ "himself is contained, offered, and received and by which the Church continually lives and grows" (c. 897). The Eucharist is "the source and summit of Christian life." All the "other sacraments, and indeed all the ministries and apostolic works of the Church are bound with the Eucharist and are oriented toward it" (*CCC,* 1324).

How was the sacrament of the Eucharist instituted in the Church?

The institution of the Eucharist is recorded in the synoptic gospels (Lk 22:14-20; Mt 26:17-29; Mk 14:12-25 and 1 Cor 11:23-26). In Mark 14:22, the evangelist wrote:

> While they were eating, Jesus took bread, blessed and broke it, and gave it to them. And he said: "Take this, this is my body." Then he took a cup and after he had given thanks, passed it to them and they all drank from it. And he said, "This is my blood, the blood of the covenant, which is to be poured out for many."

Jesus then told his apostles: "Do this in memory of me." The Church took this command seriously and it has been very faithful to the Lord's command. The members of the Church of Jerusalem devoted themselves to the teachings of the apostles and fellowship, and the breaking of bread and prayers (Acts 2:42, 46).

Who is the ordinary minister of the Eucharist?

Only a validly ordained priest or bishop, one who is in the person of Christ, can celebrate the Eucharist (c. 900). Any other member of the Catholic Church who attempts to celebrate the Eucharist incurs an automatic penalty of interdict. If a deacon attempts to celebrate the Eucharist, he incurs a penalty of suspension (c. 1378 § 2).

What is the proper form and matter for the valid celebration of the Eucharist?

The Eucharist must be offered in bread and in wine to which a small quantity of water is to be added. The bread to be offered must be of wheat and recently made, to avoid any possibility of corruption, and the wine must be naturally made from grapes of the vine (c. 924). It is absolutely wrong, even in urgent and extreme necessity, to consecrate one element without the other or to attempt to consecrate both outside the Eucharistic celebration (c. 927). The Eucharist may be received under the species of bread or wine alone or under both species of bread and wine (c. 925). The conferences of bishops are to decree the manner and how Holy Communion is to be received in their respective territories.

Who is the ordinary minister of Holy Communion?

The ordinary minister of Holy Communion is a bishop, a priest, or a deacon. A pastoral need may necessitate the institution of extraordinary ministers who help in the distribution of Holy Communion in the absence of sufficient ordinary ministers.

Who can receive Holy Communion?

Any baptized Catholic who is not forbidden by law has a right to receive Holy Communion. The Church teaches that anyone who is conscious of a grave sin is not to receive Holy Communion without previously having gone to sacramental confession, unless there is a grave reason or no opportunity to confess (c. 916). One must abstain from all forms of food and drink for at least one hour before one receives Holy Communion (c. 919 § 1). One who has received Holy Communion may receive it again on the same day when participating in a Eucharistic celebration (cc. 917; 921 § 2).

Can a Catholic minister administer Holy Communion to non-Catholic Christians?

Yes, a Catholic minister can administer Holy Communion (the Eucharist), penance, and the anointing of the sick to non-Catholic Christians under certain conditions. Canon 844 paragraphs 3 and 4 set two different conditions for non-Catholic Christians who wish to receive the sacraments of penance, the Eucharist, and the anointing of the sick. For the members of Eastern non-Catholic Churches and those churches equivalent to them, Canon 844 § 3 states that a Catholic minister may "administer the sacraments of penance, Eucharist, and anointing of the sick licitly to members of the Eastern Churches which are not in full communion with the Catholic Church, if they seek such on their own accord and are properly disposed. This is also valid for members of other Churches which in the judgment of the Apostolic

See are in the same condition in regard to the sacraments as these Eastern Churches."

The canon mentioned above addresses the question regarding the members of the Eastern non-Catholic Churches and those Churches that are equivalent to them. The Churches that are equivalent to the Eastern Orthodox Churches are: the Polish National Church, the Old Catholic Church, and the Old Roman Catholic Church, which has been singled out as having "a special place among these communions in which the Catholic traditions and institutions in part continue to exist" (Vatican II Decree on Ecumenism).

The members of these Churches may validly receive the sacraments of penance, Eucharist, and anointing of the sick from a Catholic minister under the following conditions:

- The non-Catholic Christian must ask for the sacrament on his or her own initiative. The move should not be initiated by the Catholic minister;
- It is physically impossible for the non-Catholic Christian to receive the sacrament from his or her own proper minister; and
- The person is properly disposed.

With regard to the members of ecclesial communities (that is members of the Protestant communities), paragraph 4 of canon 844 states: "If the danger of death is present or if, in the judgment of the diocesan bishop or conference of bishops, some other grave necessity urges it, a Catholic minister administers these same sacraments licitly also to other Christians not having full communion with the Catholic Church, who cannot approach a minister of their own community, and who seek on their own accord, provided that they manifest Catholic faith in respect to these sacraments and are properly disposed."

On the members of ecclesial communities, the canon sets more requirements that are to be met before they can receive these sacraments from a Catholic minister. There has to be:

- A serious need, like the danger of death or other emergency;
- The inability to approach their own minister;
- A voluntary request by the recipient;

- A manifestation of Catholic faith concerning the sacraments in questions; and
- A proper disposition to receive the sacrament.

Elucidating the requirement that the non-Catholic Christian wishing to receive any of the above-specified sacraments must manifest Catholic faith in these sacraments, Huels (2009) wrote:

> This does not mean that the person needs detailed knowledge about the theology of the sacrament in question, but only that the recipient can affirm that faith of the Church regarding these sacraments. For example, concerning the reception of the Eucharist, it suffices that the recipients believe the consecrated bread and wine is spiritual food, the body and blood of the Lord (see cc. 899 § 1; 913 § 2). For the anointing of the sick, it is sufficient that they believe that the sacrament is a spiritual means of promoting healing and comfort and if necessary, the forgiveness of sins. For penance, it is sufficient that the penitents believe that the sacrament absolves them from their sins and thus brings reconciliation with God and the Church (c. 959).

It is only baptized Christians who can be admitted to share in these sacraments; non-baptized persons cannot receive any of the sacraments.

Another question that needs to be looked at is whether Catholic Christians can receive the sacraments of penance, the Eucharist, and the anointing of the sick from a non-Catholic minister. Catholic Christians can receive these three sacraments from a non-Catholic minister whenever "necessity requires it or true spiritual advantage suggests it and provided that danger of error or of indifferentism is avoided" (c. 844 § 2). Catholic Christians can only receive the sacraments of penance, the Eucharist, and the anointing of the sick from a non-Catholic minister in whose church these sacraments are valid when "it is physically or morally impossible to approach a Catholic minister." The conditions the canon lays down are explicit and clear:

- There is explicit necessity or genuine spiritual advantage;
- There is a physical or moral impossibility of receiving the sacrament from a Catholic minister;
- There is the absence of the danger of error or indifferentism; and
- The sacrament is validly celebrated in the other Church.

The language used in laying down the above conditions is very technical and clearly discourages Catholic Christians from receiving the sacraments of penance, the Eucharist, and the anointing of the sick from Protestant ministers.

What does the term "transubstantiation" mean?

The term "transubstantiation" refers to a change or conversion of one substance into another. The term is confined to the Eucharistic rite in the Catholic Church, where it signifies the change of the entire substance of the bread and wine into the body and blood of Jesus Christ while the outward appearances of the bread and wine remain unaffected. This radical change of substance takes place when a validly ordained priest pronounces the consecratory words over the bread and wine during a Eucharistic celebration.

Though the ancient term "transubstantiation" is neither scriptural nor patristic, it expresses a Christian idea that is biblical and is evident in the writings of the Church fathers. In Matthew 26:26-28, Mark 14:22-24, Luke 22:19-20, and 1 Corinthians 11:23-28, Jesus presents bread and wine as his body and blood to his disciples and commands them: "Do this in memory of me" (Lk 22:19). Through divine omnipotence, the bread and wine cease to exist and the body and blood of Christ are made present. Thus, through the same divine power given to priests and bishops, they make Christ present when they pronounce the words of consecration over the bread and wine.

The doctrine of transubstantiation has gone through a series of theological reflections. In the second century, St. Ignatius of Antioch (d. c. 117) simply taught that the Eucharist is Christ's body. St. Justin the Martyr (d. c. 165) encouraged Christians to regard the Eucharist as the body and blood of Christ. St. Irenaeus (d. c. 207) maintained that the wine in the chalice and the bread that had been baked became the Eucharist of the Lord's body and blood. The Church fathers simply taught that the Eucharist is the body and blood of Christ without discussing how the bread and wine are changed into Christ's body and blood. The Church fathers taught that the words of Jesus Christ have power great enough to change the bread and wine into his body and blood.

However, by the fourth century, theologians such as St. Gregory of Nyssa and St. John Chrysostom began to focus more distinctly on the change itself. St. Gregory of Nyssa asserted that the bread, through consecration, is transmuted into the body of God the Word. He maintained that Christ himself effects the change through his priest. St. John Chrysostom defended the doctrine of transubstantiation when he declared: "It is not man that causes the things offered to become the body and blood of Christ, but he who was crucified for us, Christ himself. The priest, in the role of Christ, pronounces these words, but their power and grace are from God. This is my body, he says. This word transforms the things offered" (*CCC,* 1375). The Roman Council of 1079 officially and definitively declared that the bread and wine are substantially changed into the body and blood of Jesus. By the thirteenth century, the doctrine of transubstantiation had been accepted and included in the thesis of St. Thomas Aquinas that "the whole substance of the bread is changed into the whole substance of Christ's body and the whole substance of wine into the whole substance of Christ's blood" (ST. 39, 7 5, 5). The Fourth Lateran Council in 1215 and the Second Council of Lyon in 1274 used the term transubstantiation in explaining the doctrine. The Council of Florence in 1439-42 gave ample catechesis on the doctrine of transubstantiation.

Martin Luther (d. 1546) admitted and vigorously defended the real presence of Christ in the Eucharistic bread. He, however, repudiated the doctrine of transubstantiation. He believed and taught that the glorified body and blood of Christ are present "in, with, and under" the bread and wine (consubstantiation*).* John Calvin (d. 1564) rejected both transubstantiation and consubstantiation and contended that Christ's body and blood are present in the Eucharist by the power emanating from them.

On October 11, 1551, the Council of Trent issued an authoritative statement on the doctrine of transubstantiation when it declared: "It has always been the conviction of the Church of God, and this holy Council now again declares, that by the consecration of the bread and wine, a change takes place in which the entire substance of the bread is changed into the substance of the body of Christ our Lord and the entire substance of the wine is changed into the substance of his blood. This change, the holy Catholic Church fittingly and properly calls transubstantiation" (Chapter 4 of Session 13, Council of Trent).

In the *General Catechetical Directory,* the Sacred Congregation for Clergy (1971) declared that:

> When the words of consecration have been pronounced, the profound reality (but not the appearance) of bread and wine is changed into the Body and Blood of Christ. This wonderful change has been given the name *transubstantiation* in the Church. Thus it is that under the appearance that is, the phenomenal reality of bread and wine, the very humanity of Christ, not just its power, but itself, that is the substance, is hidden in a totally unfathomable way, together with his divine person. (No. 58)

In addition to his real presence in the Eucharist, Christ is also present to his Church in many other ways. Christ is present in a body of the faithful gathered in his name, for he promises to be with his disciples anytime they are gathered in his name (Mt 18:19). He is present in his Word, for it is he who speaks to his people when the Scriptures are proclaimed in the church.

What is a Mass stipend or Mass offering?

A Mass stipend is an offering that a priest or a bishop receives for celebrating a Mass. He then applies the Mass to the intention of the donor. A priest or bishop may receive an offering to offer a Mass for anyone, living and dead, Catholic and non-Catholic (cc, 901; 945). Priests are to apply a Mass to the specific intentions they have received.

What are the fruits of Holy Communion?

The worthy reception of Holy Communion enhances Christian life and thus produces a number of fruits, which include:

- An intimate union with Christ who says: "He who eats my flesh and drinks my blood abides in me and I in him" (Jn 6:56-57). Thus, our intimate union with Christ has its foundation in the Eucharist (*CCC*, 1391), and it is this union that informs and directs what we do as Christians and our ability to be the salt of the earth and the light of the world;
- The power to avoid sinning, for the body of Christ we eat is "given up for us" and his blood we drink is "shed for us and for many for the forgiveness of sins." Thus, our participation in the Eucharistic banquet brings about spiritual nourishment and cleansing from our past sins and preserves us from future sins. As physical food nourishes us and restores lost strength, so does the Eucharist strengthen our charity, which tends to be weakened by daily living. By giving himself to us in the Eucharistic banquet, Christ "revives our love and enables us to break our disordered attachment to creatures and root ourselves in him" (*CCC*, 1394; 1 Cor 10:16-17);
- Preservation from future mortal sins. As we share in the life of Christ and deepen our friendship with him, we develop an aversion to sin and grow in holiness (*CCC*, 1394); and
- Incorporation in the mystical body of Christ, the Church. It is in the light of this insight that the Catechism of the Catholic Church declares that: "Those who receive the Eucharist are united more closely to Christ. Through it, Christ unites them to all the faithful in one body—the Church. Communion renews, strengthens, and deepens this incorporation into the Church, already achieved by baptism. Because there is one bread, we who are many are one body, for we all partake of the one bread" (*CCC*, 1396).

What is the sacrament of penance?

Penance is a sacrament that enables baptized Catholics "who have fallen into grave sins and have thus lost their baptismal grace and wounded the ecclesial communion" (*CCC*, 1446) to be reconciled with Christ and his Church. Thus, penance is a sacrament by which the sinful members of the Church receive divine forgiveness and reconciliation.

Under what conditions does a penitent receive divine forgiveness?

The penitent is required to do three acts that form the matter of the sacrament: contrition, confession, and satisfaction. Confession is the "sorrow of the soul and detestation for the sins committed, together with the resolution not to sin again" (*CCC*, 1451). Contrition is said to be perfect when it arises from a love by which God is loved above all else. Such contrition brings remission of venial and mortal sins if it is backed by a firm resolution to have recourse to sacramental confession as soon as possible. It is imperfect when it arises from the fear of eternal damnation and other penalties threatening the sinner.

The penitent has to undergo a thorough examination of conscience before confessing his or her sins. The disclosure of one's sins to a priest in a confessional frees one from one's sins and facilitates one's reconciliation with God and with his Church. The disclosure of one's sins to a priest is an integral part of the sacrament of reconciliation. Having confessed his sins and received absolution, the penitent is to make satisfaction for those sins. This satisfaction is called "penance."

Who is the ordinary minister of the sacrament of penance?

The ordinary minister of confession is a priest or a bishop (c. 965). For a priest to be able to validly hear confession and to absolve a penitent, he needs a faculty or permission from the local ordinary to hear confession. A priest may be given the faculty to hear confession either by the law itself or the competent ecclesiastical authority (c. 969). The following clergymen possess the faculty to hear confession everywhere by virtue of the law itself:

- The pope and cardinals may hear confession of the faithful anywhere in the world (c. 967 § 1);
- Bishops have the faculty and may lawfully hear confession everywhere unless the diocesan bishop of a given territory denies it (c. 967 § 1);
- Pastors, local ordinaries, canon penitentiaries, those who take the place of a pastor, and chaplains may hear confession within their jurisdiction and hear the confession of their subjects even outside

of their jurisdiction, unless a diocesan bishop denies them the exercise of this right (cc. 566 § 1; 967 § 2; 968 § 1); and

- All priests, even if they lack the faculty, may hear the confession of one in danger of death (cc. 967; 1357 § 1).

What is the seal of confession?

The seal of confession is the secrecy surrounding the hearing of the sacrament of confession. The sacramental seal of confession "is inviolable; therefore it is absolutely forbidden for a confessor to betray the penitent either by words or by any other means" (c. 983 § 1). The confessor is "prohibited completely from using acquired information from the confession to the detriment of the penitent even when any danger of revelation is excluded" (c. 984 § 1). The seal of confession also binds an interpreter, if there is any in the celebration of confession. A confessor who "directly violates the sacramental seal incurs a *latae sententiae* (automatic) excommunication reserved to the Apostolic See" (c. 1338 § 1).

What is the sacrament of the anointing of the sick?

The anointing of the sick is the sacrament by which the Church "recommends to the suffering and glorified Lord the faithful who are seriously ill in order that he relieve and save them" (c. 998). The sacrament is conferred by anointing the sick with oil and pronouncing the appropriate words as prescribed by the liturgical books.

Who is the ordinary minister of the sacrament of the anointing of the sick?

Only a bishop or a priest can validly administer the anointing of the sick (c. 1003 § 1). The sacrament is conferred on any member of the Church who has reached the use of reason and has become vulnerable to the danger of death because of illness or old age (c. 1004 § 1).

What is the sacrament of holy matrimony?

Holy matrimony, a sacrament by which "a man and a woman establish between themselves a partnership of the whole of life and which is ordered by nature to the good of the spouses and the procreation and education of offspring, has been raised by Christ the Lord to the dignity of a sacrament between the baptized" (c. 1055). The essential elements highlighted in the above definition include the purpose of a Christian marriage, its properties, and its sacramentality.

What are the primary purposes of a marriage?

The purpose of a marriage is to enhance, promote the well-being of the spouses, procreate, and educate offspring. Since the ability to procreate offspring is sometimes beyond the power of the couple and remains the ultimate gift from God, the Church encourages couples to remain open to receiving this gift from God. Elucidating the ends of marriage, Beal (2000) wrote:

> To say that marriage is, by its nature, ordered to the good of the spouses and the procreation and education of offspring means that, as a natural institution, marriage has certain ends or finalities that are embedded in the nature of the institution itself (*fines operis*) and are independent of the will or the intention of the spouses (*fines operantis*). Since the achievement of the ends of marriage is somewhat beyond the power of the spouses, the failure to attain them does not in itself affect the validity of a marriage. For example, even though marriage is ordered to the procreation and education of offspring, childless marriages are presumed to be valid. However, if one or both parties exclude this essential end of marriage from their consent (i.e., refuse to give and accept the right to these ends) by a positive act of the will, they contract invalidly. (p. 1243)

What are the essential properties of a marriage?

The essential properties of marriage include unity and indissolubility. Unity in marriage refers to the ultimate union of marriage, a mutual giving of two persons to become one flesh. The indissolubility, as a property of Christian marriage, means that a marriage that has been ratified and consummated cannot be dissolved by any human power or by any cause other than death (c. 1141).

What is a sacramental marriage?

A sacramental marriage is a marriage between two baptized parties; both may be Catholics or baptized non-Catholics. The baptism of both parties can either be prior to contracting the marriage or subsequent to it. Such a marriage falls within the jurisdiction of the Church and is regulated by canon law if both parties are Catholics or even if one of the parties is a baptized non-Catholic. On the other hand, if both parties are baptized non-Catholics, the marriage laws of their Church or ecclesial community govern their marriage. If their Church or ecclesial community does not have such laws, then the laws of the state will regulate their marriage. If both parties are Catholics, but from different *Churches sui-iuris*, that is, a Latin Catholic and Eastern Catholic, then the canon laws of both Churches will be applicable.

A sacramental marriage that has not been consummated—that is, the married persons have not engaged in sexual intercourse after their marriage has been celebrated—is called *ratified* and *non-consummated. In certain cases,* the Roman Pontiff can dissolve ratified and non-consummated marriages.

What is a natural marriage?

A marriage is said to be natural if it is contracted between a baptized person and a non-baptized person or it is between two non-baptized persons. Such a marriage contracts a natural bond of marriage. If the baptized person is a Catholic Christian, then the marriage will be governed by canon law. Otherwise, the law of the state or the laws of the person's Church or ecclesial community will regulate the baptized person's marriage.

What is a mixed marriage?

A mixed marriage is a marriage contracted between a Catholic and a baptized non-Catholic or between a Catholic and a non-baptized person. The lawful celebration of the former requires permission from one's local ordinary, whereas a valid celebration of the latter requires a dispensation from the disparity of cult from one's local ordinary. The granting of permission from one's local ordinary relates to the lawfulness of the celebration, but obtaining a dispensation from the disparity of cult from one's local ordinary is required for the validity of the celebration.

Before the local ordinary grants permission or dispensation from the disparity of cult, the following conditions must be met:

- The Catholic party must declare that he or she is ready to remove any dangers of defecting from the faith and is to make a sincere promise to do all in his or her power to have all the children baptized and brought up in the Catholic Church;
- The non-Catholic is to be informed at an appropriate time about the promises that the Catholic is to make, in such a way that it is certain that he or she is truly aware of the promise and obligation of the Catholic; and
- Both parties are to be instructed about the purposes and essential properties of marriage, which neither of the contracting parties is to exclude (c. 1125).

A secret marriage: What is it?

A secret marriage is a marriage celebrated secretly without following the external requirements, such as the publication of the marriage banns or registering the marriage in a regular parish marriage register. However, a secret marriage must fulfill all requirements of the canonical form: that is, it is celebrated before an official witness of the Church and two other witnesses. The local ordinary is not to grant permission to celebrate a secret marriage unless "for a grave and urgent cause" (c. 1130) in favor of the party or parties involved.

Permission to celebrate a secret marriage implies the following:

- That the investigations that must be conducted before the marriage regarding the suitability of the parties to get married must be done in secret; and
- That the local ordinary, the one assisting at the marriage, the other witnesses, and the spouses observe secrecy about the marriage (c. 1131).

The local ordinary must be cautious about the complicity of the Church in violating the laws of the state and the danger of scandal that might arise from the spouses appearing to live together without the benefit of holy matrimony when he grants permission to celebrate a marriage secretly. The diminishing of pension income and other related benefits might be sufficient reasons for allowing secret marriages to be celebrated in one's diocese or territory. His reasons for granting permission must be far superior to the possible dangers that might arise because of his action.

What is matrimonial consent?

Matrimonial consent "is an act of the will by which a man and a woman mutually give and accept each other through an irrevocable covenant in order to establish marriage" (c. 1057 § 2). The matrimonial consent that gives rise to a valid marriage must be given and accepted by parties who have the capacity, the knowledge, and the freedom to contract marriage. The following persons are incapable of contracting valid marriage:

- Persons who lack the sufficient use of reason;
- Persons who suffer from a grave defect in judgment concerning the purpose and the essential properties of marriage; and
- Persons who, because of serious psychic illness cannot assume the essential obligations of marriage (c. 1095).

For matrimonial consent to give rise to a valid marriage, the contracting parties must not be ignorant "that marriage is a permanent partnership between a man and a woman ordered to the procreation of offspring by means of some sexual cooperation" (c. 1096 § 1).

What does the term "canonical form" of marriage mean?

Roman Catholics are required by law to marry before an official witness of the Church, such as a bishop, priest, deacon, or lawfully delegated layperson (c. 1108; c. 1127). Thus, for a marriage to be valid, it must be contracted before "the local ordinary, pastor, or a priest or deacon delegated by either one of them, who assists, and before two witnesses according to rules" (c. 1108). In the absence of a priest and deacon, the diocesan bishop can delegate a layperson to assist at marriages, if the conference of bishops has given its prior approval and the permission of the Holy See has been obtained (c. 1112 § 1). The layperson delegated to assist at marriages must be trained so that he or she can prepare couples properly and perform the matrimonial liturgy properly and effectively.

Those lawful ministers who witness marriages outside of their own territories need a special delegation from the proper pastor of the parish where the marriage is taking place; otherwise, the marriage will be invalid.

What invalidates a marriage?

The right to marry is open to all, but not everyone can contract marriage validly in the Catholic Church. Marriage, as a social and divine institution in which a man and a woman freely give and accept each other as husband and wife, is brought into being as follows:

1. The consent of the bride and the groom is given;
2. The consent is legitimately manifested; and
3. The consent is given by those who are capable or qualified according to law.

Not everyone is capable of giving the consent that precipitates a marriage. Therefore, one can conclude that some people cannot validly marry in the Church. If one who lacks the capacity to give consent gives it anyway, one is said to have a defective consent and an attempted marriage.

Defect of consent invalidates marriage because it consists of:

1. Lack of capacity (c. 1095);
2. Lack of knowledge, ignorance, error, or fraud (cc. 1096-1098); and
3. Lack of free will (cc. 1099-1103).

In addition to the defect of consent, the following diriment impediments render a person incapable of marrying validly in the Church and can invalidate a marriage:

1. Age (c. 1083, before sixteen years for a male and before fourteen for a female);
2. Prior marriage bond (c. 1085, ligament);
3. Impotence (c. 1084, it must be antecedent, that is, existing before marriage);
4. Disparity of cult (c. 1086);
5. Holy orders (c. 1087);
6. Public perpetual vow of chastity in a religious institute (c. 1088);
7. Abduction (c. 1089);
8. Crime (c. 1090);
9. Consanguinity (c. 1091);
10. Affinity (c. 1092); and
11. Public propriety (c. 1093).

A defect of canonical form also invalidates a marriage in the Church. The canonical form, that is, contracting marriage before an official witness of the Church, obliges only Catholics. The invalidity of a marriage often comes from one of the following three principal sources:

1. Existence of a diriment impediment that renders a person incapable of contracting a marriage;
2. A defect of consent of one or both persons. The matrimonial consent that creates a valid marriage must be given and received by parties who are legally capable; and

3. A defect in the required canonical form for contracting a marriage.

The diriment impediments that invalidate a marriage may be of divine origin (natural law) or of ecclesiastical law. Impediments of natural law (divine origin) bind all people, regardless of their religious affiliation. Impediments of ecclesiastical law render Roman Catholics incapable of contracting a marriage or preclude a non-Catholic who wishes to marry a Catholic.

Impediments of natural law or of divine origin include impotence, a prior valid marriage bond, and certain degrees of consanguinity, especially those involving a vertical line, such as father-daughter, or mother-son. These impediments may not be dispensed, and any marriage attempted under these circumstances is invalid.

A competent ecclesiastical authority, such as the Roman Pontiff, a diocesan bishop, or their delegates, may dispense impediments of ecclesiastical law.

What constitutes defective consent?

Defective consent results from three principal sources:
- Lack of capacity (c. 1095);
- Lack of knowledge (cc. 1096; 1097; 1098); and
- Lack of will (cc. 1098; 1101; 1102; 1103).

Lack of capacity:

Any person who lacks the capacity to give and accept consent cannot contract a valid marriage. Three elements that constitute a lack of capacity are lack of reason, lack of due discretion, and the inability to assume the essential obligations of a marriage. The parties who want to enter into a marriage must have sufficient reason to understand that marriage is a partnership of life for the good of the spouses and for the procreation and education of children. This understanding is critical for one's ability to give consent that gives rise to a valid marriage. The second element, due discretion, involves the will and the intellect to engage in a responsible human act. Two things are critical here. The parties must have the intellect to make a mature judgment and the will to freely consent to it. Due discretion also requires that the couple interested in getting married must possess the ability to critically evaluate the consequences of their decision to give themselves to each other, to be truthful to each other, and to understand and appreciate themselves as distinct individuals. The third element of the lack of capacity is the inability to assume the essential obligations of a married life.

Thus, the consent will be defective if one of the parties cannot assume the essential obligations of marriage. One of the critical duties of a marriage is the mutual exchange of the right to sexual intercourse open to the procreation of children. Thus, if one of the parties cannot engage in sexual intercourse because of impotence, the marriage will be invalid. Another critical piece of this element is the fact that "a marriage is a partnership of the whole life that by its nature is ordered toward the procreation and upbringing of children" (c. 1055).

Lack of knowledge:

The three components of a lack of knowledge are ignorance (c. 1096), error (c. 1097), and fraud (c. 1098). For a matrimonial consent to be valid, the people giving it must not be ignorant that marriage is a permanent partnership between a man and a woman for their well-being and for the procreation of children by means of sexual cooperation. Error regarding the person one is contracting a marriage with renders a marriage invalid. Malice, fraud, or deceit often blurs one's knowledge and invalidates a marriage because a person contracts a marriage invalidly if he or she "enters into a marriage by malice, perpetrated to obtain consent, concerning some quality of the other partner which by its nature can gravely disturb the partnership of conjugal life" (c. 1098). Thus, an error about a quality of the spouse can affect the consent and render the marriage invalid.

Lack of will:

Matrimonial consent is an internal act, which must be manifested in some public manner. This internal consent of the will must correspond with the words and signs employed to manifest it externally during the celebration of a marriage. When this internal will does not match what has been expressed externally, simulation is said to have taken place. Simulation invalidates matrimonial consent and thus renders a marriage invalid. Other critical elements that undermine the will are conditional consent (c. 1102) and force and fear (c. 1103).

Diriment impediments: What are they?

Diriment impediments are facts or circumstances that render a person incapable of contracting a valid marriage in the Church. An impediment is public if it can be proven in the external forum; otherwise, it is occult (c. 1074). An impediment may be of divine law, in which case it binds everyone, Catholics and non-Catholics. Impotence is an impediment of divine law, and therefore an impotent person is incapable of contracting a valid marriage. Impediments of merely ecclesiastical law bind only Catholics and a non-Catholic who wishes to marry a Catholic.

Can an invalid marriage be validated?

Yes, an invalid marriage can be validated in one of the following ways:

1. By simple validation or convalidation (c. 1156), that is, a legal remedy by which a previous invalid marriage is made valid. This procedural remedy may be simple convalidation or *sanatio in radice.*
2. By a new celebration of the marriage using the proper required canonical form once the invalidating impediment or defect ceases, or if the invalidity arises from a defect of canonical form (c. 1160); and
3. By a canonical process called *sanatio in radice* (retroactive validation). In this process, the parties need not renew their marital consent; it is done through the action of a competent ecclesiastical authority removing the obstacle and thus making the marriage valid (c. 1160).

The Church Tribunal: What is it?

The term "Church tribunal" refers to Church courts that try cases at the request of, and on behalf of, individuals seeking justice in the Church. The goal of these ecclesiastical courts is to pursue or vindicate rights, to declare legal facts, or impose penalties. The ecclesiastical courts form part of the healing ministry of the Church. In her judicial function, the Church comes in direct contact with those individuals, both Catholics and non-Catholics, whose lives have been deeply wounded by the bitter experience of a broken marriage or any other gross injustice. Through the pursuit of justice and forgiveness, the Church courts try to heal and reconcile those who feel alienated from the Body of Christ and are burdened with a great deal of pain.

Like the civil courts, the ecclesiastical courts are categorized into lower and superior courts. The lower courts are the first and second instance tribunals. The first instance tribunals are the diocesan tribunals. The second instance tribunals are general tribunals comprised of a number of dioceses, and they are usually appeal courts at the lower level (cc. 1438-41).

The superior courts are the Tribunal of the Roman Rota and the Supreme Tribunal of the Apostolic Signatura. Both tribunals are courts of the Apostolic See. The Tribunal of the Roman Rota is the highest court of appeal in the Catholic Church, while the Supreme Tribunal of the Apostolic Signatura has universal oversight for the judicial system in the Church. It is like a department of justice for the Catholic Church.

Unlike the civil courts, which try persons, the Church tribunals try cases. The parties involved in a trial present their cases separately. The tribunal staff gathers any relevant testimony and consults experts, and then the defender of the bond and the promoter of justice study the evidence and document their comments and concerns. The judges study the acts and evidence presented to them, and then they render a decision on the case.

Generally, when we speak of a Church tribunal, the tribunal that handles marriage cases is the obvious one that comes to mind. There is another type of Church tribunal called the administrative tribunal. An administrative tribunal is "a judicial forum in which a panel of judges adjudicates claims that an administrative decision violated the law, either because the procedure followed was defective or because the grounds on which it was based were erroneous." Thus, an administrative tribunal is one of the possible options Catholic Christians have for administrative recourse. The other option is a hierarchic recourse. The administrative tribunal is part of the Supreme Tribunal of the Apostolic Signatura and handles all administrative acts that violate individual rights (*PB*, 123).

The role of a tribunal that deals with marriage cases, according to Pope Pius XI, is "to care for the dignity of marriage and to work for the good of the person." In the pursuance of these objectives, the tribunals are to use the teachings of Jesus Christ as recorded in the Holy Scripture and Church law as their guidelines. A tribunal normally handles marriage cases, studying and examining the cases presented to it, and then declares a legal fact regarding the status of the marriage in question. In studying and examining cases, a tribunal tries to answer the following questions: Were the parties prevented from being married because of any diriment impediments? Were the parties capable of giving and accepting matrimonial consent at the time they exchanged it? Did they have the required knowledge? Did they have the will to enter into a valid marriage? Did they fulfill all the requirements of the canonical form?

Is there any difference between an annulment and a divorce?

An annulment is quite different from a divorce. The Catholic Church teaches that marriage validly celebrated and consummated is *indissoluble*, which means that it cannot be terminated. Thus, marriage creates a perpetual relationship between a man and a woman, which cannot be terminated by any human being.

The difference between divorce and annulment is that while divorce terminates a marriage, an annulment declares that a marriage never existed in the first place. The Catholic Church treats civil divorces, which often adjudicate child custody and the division of property, as mere legal separations. Divorced Catholics are seen as still being married to one another because of the existence of an indissoluble marriage bond between the spouses. Divorced Catholics are still in full communion with the Church and can fully participate in the sacramental life of the Church until one of them or both attempt another marriage. The existing marital bond between the spouses will invalidate the attempted marriage in the eyes of the Church. The spouses can remain separated until one of them dies.

Two people validly married in the Church could not have children: Can their inability to procreate be grounds for nullifying their marriage?

The purpose of marriage as stated in canon 1055 § 1 is that marriage is ordered by its nature toward the well-being of the spouses and the procreation and education of children. It is true that procreation is an essential purpose of a marriage. However, in some cases, procreation is beyond the ability of the spouses. The Catholic Church teaches that children are gifts from God and they are to be received with thanks and open arms. Therefore, the inability to procreate cannot be grounds for nullifying one's marriage. However, if one of the parties excludes the intention to procreate at the time of marriage, then that exclusion can be grounds for nullifying the marriage.

Why does the Catholic Church have these tribunals to adjudicate cases when our civil courts can perform these functions?

The Catholic Church has a proper and exclusive right to adjudicate cases that relate to spiritual matters or those connected to the spiritual well-being of her children as well as cases that violate ecclesiastical law and all other acts that relate to sin in what pertains to the determination of culpability and the imposition of ecclesiastical penalty. This right of the Church to adjudicate cases can be traced to the exhortation of St. Paul when he declared:

> How can anyone with a case against another dare to bring it
> for judgment to the wicked and not to God's holy people?
> Do you not know that the believers will judge the world?
> If the judgment of the world is yours, are you to be thought
> unworthy of judging in minor matters? Do you not know that
> we are to judge angels? Surely, then, we are up to deciding
> every-day affairs. If you have such matters to decide, why

do you accept as judges those who have no standing in the Church? I say this in an attempt to shame you. Can it be that there is no one among you wise enough to settle a case between one member of the Church and another? Must brother drag brother into court, and before unbelievers at that? (1 Cor 6: 1-6)

St. Paul, in the above passage, seems to suggest the establishment of some kind of court system to settle conflicts or disputes that might arise among the early Christian community. The ecclesiastical courts use the teachings of Jesus Christ as recorded in the Gospels as their guidelines when adjudicating cases brought before these courts. Tertullian, in the thirty-ninth chapter of his *Apology*, argues that Christians have high moral standards when settling disputes among themselves. Roman Emperor Constantine granted the bishops of the Church the same authority as civil judges to hear and settle cases brought before them by the mutual consent of the parties. The pope is the supreme judge of the universal Church. He exercises his judicial power through the judges he appoints to adjudicate cases in his name. In each diocese, the diocesan bishop is the chief judge. Each diocesan bishop constitutes a diocesan tribunal to assist him in the adjudication of cases arising from among the members in his local church. The Church has these courts to settle cases as suggested by St. Paul in the above quoted passage.

Each diocesan bishop is to appoint a judicial vicar, who handles judicial matters in the name of the bishop. The judicial vicar is to be given ordinary power to judge all cases except those the bishop reserves to himself or those cases reserved to the Apostolic See. Thus, every diocese is to have its own tribunal. With the approval of the Apostolic See, several diocesan bishops can jointly establish a first instance tribunal and also tribunals of appeal to handle all marriage cases arising from these dioceses. The diocesan bishop or bishops, after erecting a regional tribunal with the approval of the Apostolic See, appoint one judicial vicar, a number of judges, a defender of the bond, a promoter of justice, and other personnel to assist the judicial vicar in the adjudication of cases brought before the regional tribunal.

The object of a Church tribunal trial, according to canon 1400 § 1, is "the pursuit or vindication of the rights of physical or juridical persons or the declaration of juridical facts, the imposition or declaration of a penalty for delicts." In canon law, a physical person is an individual person with rights and obligations in the Church. There are five key elements: age, mental condition, residence, legal relationship, and rite, which qualify the status of persons in the Church. The legal system of the Catholic Church has created artificial entities such as parishes, dioceses, religious institutes, societies of apostolic life, conferences of bishops, seminaries, hospitals, and Catholic universities. These entities are known as juridical persons in canon law.

The Church tribunals pursue two kinds of trials: contentious and penal. The tribunal pursues contentious trials to vindicate the rights of persons or to declare juridical facts. Contentious cases that a Church tribunal handles include cases that concern the bond of sacred ordination or the bond of marriage. The penal cases that the Church tribunal handles include cases concerning delicts, which entail the penalty of dismissal from the clerical state or cases that relate to the imposition or declaration of an excommunication.

Controversies often arise from the administrative acts of bishops, superiors, or their delegates, and their subjects can be aggrieved by these actions of administrative powers. Administrative tribunals handle such controversies. For instance, a priest who is aggrieved by the administrative action of his bishop or superior cannot take recourse against the bishop's action in any ordinary Church tribunal. The case usually starts in a congregation and may end up in the Signatura. The administrative tribunal of the Apostolic Signatura is the appropriate office that handles these cases. Since the administrative tribunal is part of the Supreme Tribunal of the Apostolic Signatura, and not universally available like the tribunals that handle marriage cases, the Church recommends the establishment of hierarchic recourse centers to handle administrative actions that may violate the rights of individuals at the diocesan or national level (c. 1733 § 2).

The Church preaches forgiveness and exhorts its members to forgive those who wrong them: Why then does the Church often punish its errant members?

The Church has "its own innate and proper right to coerce offending members of the Christian faithful with penal sanctions" (c. 1311). The Church's right to punish its errant members is in line with the advice St. Paul gives to Timothy when he exhorts him to "rebuke publicly all those who commit sins, so that the rest may be afraid" (1 Tm 5:20). Explaining the reasons for the penal sanctions in the Catholic Church and why errant members must be punished, Woestman (2000) declared "the Church's right and obligation to punish its errant members flows from its nature as a visible community or society and the consequent necessity to recall sinners to their Christian duty and repentance, to protect the innocent faithful from bad examples and behavior disruptive of ecclesial communion, to promote the unity of faith, and to deter the weak from being led astray" (p. 7).

The sanctions that the Church often applies to its errant members are either medicinal censures or expiatory penalties. The medicinal censures that are applied to errant members of the Church discourage sinful behavior that may be harmful to individual members and may disrupt ecclesial communion. Examples of medicinal censures are excommunication, interdict, and suspension. While excommunication and interdict may be imposed on any member of the Church, suspension is only imposed on errant clerics to totally or partially restrict their liturgical and pastoral ministry. Errant members who are punished by medicinal censures are deprived of access to the sacraments and ecclesiastical office until they are restored in ecclesial communion. For instance, an excommunicated member is forbidden to:

- Have any ministerial participation in celebrating the sacrifice of the Eucharist or any other ceremonies of worship whatsoever;
- Celebrate the sacraments or sacramentals and receive the sacraments; and

- Exercise any ecclesiastical offices, ministries, or functions whatsoever or perform acts of governance (c. 1331 § 1).

Clerics who are suspended are forbidden to exercise all or some of the powers of holy orders. Suspension may prevent a cleric from holding an ecclesiastical office in the Church.

Expiatory penalties are more punitive in nature than censures because they aim at repairing the societal damage caused by the behavior or action of the errant members. Unlike censures, expiatory penalties do not require a prior warning before they are imposed. These penalties may be perpetual, as dismissal from the clerical state or for a definite period of time; for example, a bishop may be forbidden to confer sacred orders for a year (c. 1383).

From the aforementioned, one can conclude that the Church punishes its errant members not because it does not believe in forgiveness, but in order to bring about conformity and to ensure compliance. As a societal community, the Church needs laws and regulations to ensure that its members conform to its core beliefs and teachings. When its errant members repent of their erroneous teachings and errant ways and display a spirit of conversion, the Church always remits any imposed censures and penalties and accepts them into full communion. Thus, these censures, penalties, and other punishments that the Church imposes on its errant members are remedies to ensure ecclesial unity and conformity to its core doctrines.

CHAPTER 6

Catholic Beliefs and Practices

In this chapter, questions about Catholic beliefs and practices are discussed. In so doing the focus would be on sacramentals, the liturgy of the hours, funerals, the devotion to saints and sacred images, sacred places, and other practices that are exclusively Catholic.

What are sacramentals? How are they different from the sacraments?

The Second Vatican Council describes sacramentals as "sacred signs which bear a resemblance to the sacraments. They signify effects, particularly of a spiritual nature, which are obtained through the Church's intercession" (SC, 60). Some examples of sacramentals are the rite of blessing, the dedication of churches, the consecration of altars, the consecration of virgins and chrism, exorcism, religious profession, the institution of ministries such as lectors and acolytes, the crowning of the images of the Blessed Virgin Mary, and blessed objects such as holy water, blessed candles, blessed palms or ashes, blessed medals, and blessed scapulars.

The celebration of sacramentals often brings about the reality of sacredness and confers spiritual comfort and security to the lives of Catholic Christians. For instance, a pregnant woman may find spiritual comfort in a sacramental, such as a blessing before she goes into labor or the wearing of scapulars may precipitate spiritual comfort and security to some Catholic Christians. The Apostolic See is the sole authority that "can establish new sacramentals, authentically interpret those already received, or abolish or change any of them" (c. 1167 § 1).

A cleric is a proper minister of sacramentals. In conferring or administering a sacramental, the minister must carefully follow

the proper rites and formulas approved by the Church (c. 1167 §
2). A local ordinary may in certain cases permit a properly trained
layperson who possesses the necessary qualities to administer some
sacramentals. For instance, a layperson may be allowed to administer
ashes to the faithful on Ash Wednesday for pastoral reasons.

A bishop is the proper minister of those sacramentals that are
marked with episcopal character, such as dedication and consecration.
A priest may administer a dedication or consecration only when
permitted by law or by special concession as stated in canon 1206:
"The dedication of any place belongs to the diocesan bishop and
to those equivalent to him by law. They can entrust the function
of carrying out a dedication in their territory to any bishop or, in
an exceptional case, to a presbyter." Objects that are consecrated,
dedicated, or blessed are to be accorded the reverence they deserve and
are not to be profaned or used inappropriately.

A deacon can impart only those blessings that are expressly
permitted by law. For instance, the law permits a deacon to impart
blessings when he presides over liturgical celebrations, such as the
liturgy of hours, baptism, marriage, Holy Communion service, or
when he administers viaticum outside Mass.

Sacramentals are similar to the sacraments, because like the
sacraments, the sacramentals are sacred signs or objects that produce
some spiritual effects or benefit. However, they are different from
sacraments because:

a. While sacraments were instituted by Christ, sacramentals are
    instituted by the Apostolic See;
b. While sacraments have a divine origin and cannot be abolished
    or changed, sacramentals can be suppressed, abolished, or
    changed, and a competent ecclesiastical authority can institute
    new ones; and
c. While sacraments produce their spiritual effects *ex opera
    operato,* that is, through the action itself, sacramentals produce
    effects through the intercession of the Church.

A blessing as a sacramental is to be imparted first to Catholics. It
may be given to catechumens and even non-Catholic Christians, unless
Church law says otherwise.

Exorcisms are another type of sacramental by which an exorcist asks the Lord to expel a demon spirit from a person, an object, or an animal. The Catechism of the Catholic Church describes exorcism as a sacramental by which "the Church asks publicly and authoritatively in the name of Jesus Christ that a person or an object be protected against the power of the evil one and be withdrawn from his dominion" (CCC, no. 1673).

The proper minister of exorcism is a priest. The minister of exorcism must have piety, knowledge, prudence, and integrity of life. No one is to "perform exorcism legitimately upon the possessed unless he has obtained special and express permission from the local ordinary" (c. 1172 § 1). Some dioceses appoint a priest as a diocesan exorcist who performs exorcism cases in their territories.

The Liturgy of the Hours: What is it?

The liturgy of the hours, also known as "divine office," is a form of prayer "that has been consistently celebrated by the Church since ancient times, and together with the Eucharist, it remains today the principal form of daily prayer throughout the Church" (Huels, 2000, p. 1406). Through this form of prayer, the Church "hears God speaking to his people and recalling the mystery of salvation, praises him without ceasing by song and prayer and intercedes for the salvation of the whole world" (c. 1173).

This prayer consists of scriptural psalms, readings, and canticles. The prayer is said at various hours of the day, and in so doing, the whole course of the day and night is sanctified by the praises of God. Through this form of prayer, the Church fulfills the Lord's precept to "pray without ceasing."

Since the main purpose of the liturgy of hours is to sanctify the whole day, it is celebrated at certain specified times of the day when possible. The Morning Prayer, *lauds,* and the Evening Prayer, *Vespers,* are the two hinges on which the liturgy of the hours turn. The Morning Prayer is celebrated at any time before 9:00 a.m. and the Evening Prayer is celebrated in late afternoon at 4:00 p.m. In addition to the morning and evening prayers, there is mid-morning prayer, midday prayer, mid-afternoon prayer, and night prayer. The mid-morning prayer is celebrated at 9:00 a.m.; midday prayer is said at noon, the mid-afternoon prayer is celebrated at 3:00 p.m., and the night prayer is said any time after 8:00 p.m. or any time before one goes to bed.

Priests and transitional deacons are obliged to celebrate the liturgy of hours daily. Permanent deacons are to celebrate parts of the liturgy of the hours at some specified times as decided by the conference of bishops in a given territory. Seminarians are "to be formed in the celebration of the liturgy of the hours" (c. 246 § 2) so that they can inculcate this habit of praying to God in the name of the Church for all people and for the whole world. Since this form of prayer is one of the means for pursuing holiness, the lay faithful are encouraged to participate in the celebration of the liturgy of hours.

Why does the Catholic Church attach great importance to funeral Masses?

The Roman Catholic Church attaches importance to ecclesiastical funerals and recommends that funerals be celebrated for the dead because "the Church seeks spiritual support for the deceased, honors their bodies, and at the same time brings the solace of hope to the living" (c. 1176 § 2). In celebrating ecclesiastical funerals, the Church prays for the deceased person, honoring his or her body with respect, because the body was consecrated in baptism, reaffirming the Church's belief in the Resurrection and comforting the bereaved family. The celebration of a Christian funeral serves three purposes, which are:

- Praying for the soul of the dead person, asking the Lord to be merciful in judging him or her so that he or she may be counted among his chosen ones. The Church pleads with the merciful God that as the deceased person's faith united him or her to God's people on earth, so may his divine mercy join him or her to the saints in heaven;
- Honoring the body of the deceased person; the Church treats dead bodies with respect. The Catholic Church allows cremation, provided it is not chosen contrary to the Church's belief and teaching regarding the Resurrection (c. 1184). The Church law does not address the issues of autopsies and organ donations that may be done for scientific purposes; and

- Seeking to bring comfort and consolation to the living and to strengthen the belief of the bereaved that death is not the end of life, but only a transition. This belief is expressed and manifested in the fact that ecclesiastical funerals are celebrated in an atmosphere full of faith, hope, and respect.

Catholic Christians have a right to a Christian funeral. Catechumens are counted among the Catholic faithful and thus have a right to an ecclesiastical funeral. The local ordinary may allow children, whom their parents intended to baptize but who died before baptism, to be given a Christian funeral (c. 1183 § 2). The local ordinary, after prudent judgment, may grant ecclesiastical funerals to baptized non-Catholic Christians. This should not be done against the wishes of the family of the deceased person (c. 1183 § 3). Ecclesiastical funerals are not to be given to the following persons:

- Notorious apostates, heretics, and schismatics, unless they exhibit signs of repentance before death. An indication of repentance would include summoning a priest at the time of death, confessing one's sin during the last moments of life, making an act of contrition, or making a sign of the cross in the absence of a priest;
- Those who choose the cremation of their bodies for reasons contrary to the Christian faith; and
- Other people who cannot be given a church funeral without creating a public scandal among the Catholic faithful (c. 1184).

The funeral of a Christian is to be celebrated in the deceased person's proper parish church. A diocesan bishop is to be celebrated in his Cathedral unless he has chosen another church (c. 1178). Funerals of titular bishops may be celebrated in the cathedral unless the diocesan bishop decides otherwise or the deceased titular bishop had made another provision regarding the place for his funeral. Catholic Christians are allowed to choose the place where they want to be buried.

Why does the Catholic Church allow the veneration of saints, relics, and sacred images?

The Catholic Church believes and teaches that human life is changed but not ended by death, because in death, the righteous members gain an everlasting dwelling in heaven. These righteous members are called the saints, who are believed to have gained an everlasting dwelling place in the presence of God. The word "saint" is from the Latin word *sanctus,* which means "a holy one." In Catholic tradition, saints are viewed as specially blessed members of the Church who were chosen by God and had followed the example of Christ more closely and gave outstanding testimony to the Kingdom of heaven by shedding their blood or by the heroic practice of virtues (Pope John Paul II DPM, 1983). The saints are thus viewed as "friends of God and soldiers of Christ Jesus," who defended and preserved the Catholic faith. Before delving into why the Church allows the veneration of saints, let us examine the procedure by which the Church declares someone a saint.

One is officially declared a saint in the Church through a process known as "canonization." The present procedures of canonization in the Church date back to the seventeenth century. The procedure is regulated by canon law (c. 1403 § 2), the Apostolic Constitution of Pope John Paul II, *Divinus Prefectionis Magister,* January 25, 1983, and the Congregation for the Causes of Saints.

The process of declaring someone a saint consists of two stages: beatification and canonization. The introductory phase is the investigative stage, which is normally begun at a diocesan level by a diocesan bishop. The diocesan bishop has the right and obligation to conduct an inquiry about the life, virtues, reputation of sanctity or martyrdom, alleged miracles, and the general virtuous life of the person whose canonization is being sought. The diocesan bishop usually appoints a special commission to meticulously undertake an investigative study of the life of the person to be named a saint, and the commission works closely with the Congregation for the Causes of Saints. If the commission finds enough evidence testifying that the person deserves to be honored with the elects, he or she is beatified and declared *blessed* in the Church.

The commission continues with its study on the acts and deeds of the beatified person until it finds indisputable miracles associated with the person. The commission submits its findings and recommendation to the Congregation for the Causes of Saints. The congregation carefully studies the acts and findings from the commission and if it finds enough evidence, it makes a recommendation to the Supreme Pontiff, who then declares the beatified person a saint in a solemn ceremony known as *canonization* (Pope John Paul II, *DPM,* 1983). Only the Supreme Pontiff can grant official recognition to a person to be declared *blessed* and eventually *a saint.*

The church authorizes public veneration and devotion to the saints because it has always believed that the apostles, martyrs, and the saints "are closely united with us in Christ . . . and has venerated them together with the Blessed Virgin Mary and the holy angels with special love and has asked piously for the help of their intercession" (*LG,* 50). The Church always encourages her members to venerate the saints, because it believes that "when we consider the life of those who have faithfully followed Christ, we are inspired with a new reason to seek the City that is to come and we are most safely taught the path by which, amid the changing things of this world and in keeping with the stated in life and condition proper to each of us, we can arrive at that perfect union with Christ, which is holiness. Surrounded as we are by such an array of witnesses through whom God is present to us and speaks to us, we are powerfully drawn to reach His Kingdom in heaven" (Pope John Paul II, *DPM,* 1983). Through such veneration and devotion to the saints, the Church believes these righteous members will assist the pilgrim Church and its individual members on their way to perfection. Since those declared as saints of the Church are still members of the Church, and victorious members of the Church, they can offer some special favors, such as curing the sick, helping the Catholic faithful defeat their enemies, helping them excel, spurring them on their pursuit of holiness, and interceding for the living.

The Catholic Church believes that the saints have gained admittance to the heavenly kingdom and are in the divine presence (*CCC,* 947). They can intercede for their brothers and sisters who struggle with sin. This is the rationale for the veneration of the saints in the Church. Catholics do not worship the saints. The saints are the victorious members of the Church, and since they have been through the challenges of everyday living, the Church asks them to pray for its members. The Church further encourages its members to look to the saints as models of Christian living and to draw inspiration and strength from their example.

The devotion of relics is one of the most popular forms of the veneration of the saints in the Catholic tradition (c. 1190 § 2). Relics are objects associated with a particular saint. Relics can be, for example, the clothing of a saint, a part of a saint's body, such as an arm, forearm, heart, tongue, leg, or any part of a martyr's body (Huels, 2000). There are different forms of the veneration of saints' relics. Some churches, shrines, and basilicas were built on the tombs of saints, and these may attract different kinds of devotional practices in the Church.

Sacred images, such as crucifixes, statues of the Blessed Virgin Mary, and statutes of the saints in Catholic churches are not objects of worship, but a constant reminder to those who enter these churches that they are in a sacred environment illuminated by the light of faith, hope, and the redeeming divine presence (CCE, 1988, no. 25). For instance, the sacred images of Christ Jesus are in Catholic churches to remind everyone who enters these churches of the familiar and moving presence of Christ Jesus, who gave his most complete and sublime love on the Cross for the salvation of humankind.

What is the difference between a church and a chapel?

A church is "a sacred building designated for divine worship to which the faithful have the right of entry for the exercise, especially the public exercise, of divine worship" (c. 1214). An example of a church includes a parish church or a cathedral. A chapel, on the other hand, is a place "designated for divine worship by the permission of the local ordinary for the benefit of one or more physical persons" (c. 1226). Examples of a chapel include places of worship in seminaries, Catholic universities, religious houses, and houses of formation.

The basic difference between a church and a chapel is that:

- While the general Catholic faithful have the right of entry to a church to exercise public worship, the Catholic faithful do not have the right of entry to a chapel, except for those for whom the chapel was built; and

- While a church is subject to the authority and oversight of the diocesan bishop, a chapel is under the authority and supervision of the religious order or the physical persons that own the chapel.

What is a shrine?

A shrine is a church or other sacred place to which, because of some special piety, the Catholic faithful make pilgrimages with the approval of a competent ecclesiastical authority. Two essential elements in the notion of a shrine are:

1. It is a sacred place; and
2. The local ordinary has approved it for the purpose of devotional practices, such as pilgrimages.

For a place to be sacred, a competent ecclesiastical authority must designate the place for divine worship or for the burial of the departed faithful and must dedicate or bless the place following the prescribed liturgical rites (c. 1205).

A shrine may be diocesan, national, or international. A diocesan shrine is a sacred place designated and approved by the diocesan bishop for the people in his diocese to make pilgrimages to (c. 1231 § 1). For a shrine to be called a national shrine, the bishops' conference must approve it as such. An international shrine is a shrine approved and designated by the Holy See as a sacred place for divine worship for the universal Church.

The bishops' conference and the Holy See, respectively, approve the statutes of national and international shrines. The statutes of a shrine spell out its purpose, the authority of the rector, the ownership, and the administration of the temporal goods of the shrine (c. 1231 § 2). The competent ecclesiastical authority who erects and designates a shrine as a sacred place for devotional practices may grant it special privileges, such as special indulgences and the performance of some specified parochial functions.

What is a basilica?

The word "basilica" is derived from a Greek word that means "a royal house." The term "basilica" as used in the Catholic Church is a title the pope assigns to more important churches. These churches enjoy privileges of an honorific character. Thus, a basilica is a church that is renowned within a given diocese. Such a church may have been built on a certain historical site or dedicated on the occasion of some important religious event or else contains the relic of a saint.

There are two kinds of basilicas: major or papal basilicas and minor basilicas. The major basilicas are St. John Lateran Basilica, St. Peter's Basilica, St. Paul's Outside the Walls Basilica, and St. Mary Major Basilica. These four major basilicas are all in Rome.

- St. John's Lateran Basilica is the Cathedral of the Pope, the Patriarch of the West;
- St. Peter's Basilica is assigned to the Patriarch of Constantinople;
- St. Paul's Outside the Walls Basilica is assigned to the Patriarch of Alexandria; and
- St. Mary Major Basilica is assigned to the Patriarch of Antioch.

The minor basilicas are important churches in many dioceses throughout the world. Once a church is designated as a basilica by the pope, it is always a basilica.

A cathedral is the most important church in a given diocese because it holds the throne of the diocesan bishop. A cathedral may also be a basilica depending on the decision of the diocesan bishop. For instance, St. John Lateran Basilica is also the cathedral church of the Bishop of Rome.

What are the holy days of obligation in the Church?

Holy days of obligation are special days the church sets aside for the solemn celebration of the Holy Eucharist, and the Catholic faithful are obliged to observe them and to abstain from work. The Catholic Church celebrates the death and Resurrection of Jesus Christ on Sunday, and Catholics are obliged to actively participate in such a solemn celebration. Thus, Sunday, the day of the Lord on which, by apostolic tradition, the Holy Eucharist is celebrated, "must be observed in the universal Church as the primordial holy day of obligation" (c. 1246 § 1). Besides Sunday, the following dates are holy days of obligation in the Latin Church:

- January 1 (the feast of Holy Mary, Mother of God);
- January 6 (the feast of Epiphany);
- The sixth Thursday after Easter (the feast of the Ascension);
- The Thursday after the feast of the Blessed Trinity (Corpus Christi; the feast of the Body and Blood of Christ);
- March 19 (the Solemnity of St. Joseph, the husband of Mary);
- June 29 (the feast of Saints Peter and Paul);
- August 15 (the feast of the Assumption);
- November 1 (the feast of All Saints);
- December 8 (the feast of the Immaculate Conception); and
- December 25 (Christmas).

The law requires that December 25 (Christmas) and January 1 (the Solemnity of Holy Mary, the Mother of God) be observed in every country.

Observing all ten of the holy days of obligation is likely to create some inconveniences among the Catholic faithful because of time demands, so the law authorizes the bishops' conferences in various countries to suppress the obligations of some and transfer others to Sundays. Bishops' conferences in different countries need confirmation from the Apostolic See to effectively suppress the obligation of a holy day or transfer it to Sunday. Bishops' conferences are further authorized to retain those feasts that are not transferred to Sunday on their proper feast day. They can abolish the obligation to attend Mass and abstain from work. For instance, in the United States, the feasts of Epiphany and the Body and Blood of Christ are transferred to Sunday, while the feasts of St. Joseph (March 19) and Saints Peter and Paul are retained on their proper feast days, but the obligation to attend Mass and abstain from work has been suppressed.

The Catholic faithful are obliged to observe Sunday and other holy days of obligation by participating in the Eucharistic celebration and abstaining from all forms of work. The obligation is fulfilled when one is physically and consciously present at a Eucharistic celebration and has observed the day of rest. Those people whose livelihood requires them to work on Sundays and other holy days of obligation are morally excused from the observance of rest. The Catholic faithful who find it physically and morally impossible to attend Sunday liturgy are morally excused without seeking dispensation from their local ordinary. Those Catholics who cannot participate in a Eucharistic celebration because of the absence of a sacred minister can fulfill the Sunday obligation by participating in the liturgy of the word if their diocesan bishop allows such celebrations (see *Directory for Sunday Celebrations in the Absence of Presbyter,* issued by the Congregation of Divine Worship, 1988).

What is an ecumenical council? Does an ecumenical council have any significance?

The word "ecumenical" is derived from the Greek word *oikoumene,* which means "universal" as pertains to the whole world. The term "ecumenical council" as used in the Church refers to a gathering of bishops to discuss matters significant to the universal Church. Such a gathering has significant importance for the universal Church. Scholars unanimously consider the Council of Nicaea in 325 as the first ecumenical council. The ecumenicity of a council is determined by the following criteria set by the Second Council of Nicaea in 753:

- The five patriarchal sees, particularly the See of Rome, must participate in the council personally or through a lawful ecclesiastical delegate;
- The decisions of the council must be accepted by the whole Church; and
- The council teachings must be in agreement with those of previous councils whose ecumenicity was accepted by the universal Church.

Huels (2001) spoke of the horizontal and vertical consensus that is critical in determining the ecumenicity of a council. The horizontal consensus is the acceptance of the acts and decrees by the whole Church, while the vertical consensus determines whether the acts and decrees of the council are in agreement with the apostolic tradition.

While the Latin Church puts more emphasis on the participation of the Bishop of Rome in determining the ecumenicity of a council, the Eastern Church emphasizes the importance of the participation of all the patriarchal sees: Rome, Alexandria, Antioch, Constantinople, and Jerusalem.

In recent years, however, the Latin Church has relied heavily on papal participation and the approval of a council's decrees to determine its ecumenicity. For instance, the 1917 Code of Canon Law maintains that the ecumenicity of a council depends on the participation of the Supreme Pontiff and his approval of its decisions.

Presently, when the Church speaks of ecumenical councils, it refers to the first seven major councils that were accepted by the whole Church, east and west, and the general councils of the Roman Catholic Church. The following are the ecumenical councils of the Catholic Church:

1. Council of Nicaea I   325
2. Council of Constantinople I   381
3. Council of Ephesus   431
4. Council of Chalcedon   451
5. Council of Constantinople II   553
6. Council of Constantinople III   680-681
7. Council of Nicaea II   787
8. Council of Constantinople IV   869-870
9. Council of Lateran I   1123
10. Council of Lateran II   1139
11. Council of Lateran III   1179
12. Council of Lateran IV   1215
13. Council of Lyons I   1245
14. Council of Lyons II   1274
15. Council of Vienne   1311-1312
16. Council of Constance   1414-1418
17. Council of Basel-Ferrara-Florence-Rome 1431-1437 (at Basel)
                                            1438-1439 (at Ferrara)
                                            1439-1442 (at Florence)
                                            1442-1445 (at Rome)
18. Council of Lateran V   1512-1517
19. Council of Trent   1545-1563

20. Council of Vatican I   1869-1870
21. Council of Vatican II   1962-1965

These ecumenical councils are significant in many respects because they helped to define doctrines that are critical to the Christian faith. In the following, some of the major doctrines that were definitively defined by some of these councils are highlighted by illustrating the importance of each of these councils.

1. The First Council of Nicaea (325).
    a. The council fathers repudiated Arianism. They formulated and adopted the original Nicene Creed. They granted Jerusalem a position of honor.
2. The First Council of Constantinople (381).
    a. The council fathers revised the Nicene Creed into its present form. The council decreed that no further changes be made to the Creed without the assent of an ecumenical council;
3. Council of Ephesus (431).
    a. The Council of Ephesus repudiated Nestorianism and then proclaimed the Blessed Virgin Mary as *Theotokos*, which means *God-bearer* or simply the Mother of God.
4. The Council of Chalcedon (451).
    a. The council fathers rejected the doctrine of *monophysitism* and taught that Jesus Christ is truly man and God. He has two natures, divine and human. The Third Council of Constantinople (680-681) reaffirmed that Jesus Christ has both human and divine natures.
5. The Second Council of Nicaea (787).
    a. The council fathers promoted the veneration of icons. This council was the last council that the whole Church accepted as ecumenical. After this council, the bishops of the Latin Church mostly attended the general councils and the Church in the East did not accept their decisions.
6. The Second Lateran Council (1139).
    a. The council decreed that clerical marriages were invalid, thereby promoting clerical celibacy in the Latin Church, and they also issued decrees about clerical dress. The

council further decreed that physical attacks on clerics are punishable by excommunication.

7. The Third Lateran Council (1179).
   a. The council decreed that only cardinals have the exclusive right to elect the Supreme Pontiff. The council condemned simony and further decreed that no one is to be promoted to the episcopate before his thirtieth birthday.

8. The Fourth Lateran Council (1215).
   a. The council dealt with the doctrine of transubstantiation (how the Eucharistic bread and wine changes into the body and blood of Christ), papal primacy, and the rightful conduct of the clergy.

9. The First Council of Lyon (1245).
   a. The council fathers mandated the wearing of a red hat for cardinals. The council also decreed a levy for the Holy Land.

10. The Second Council of Lyon (1274).
    a. The council attempted to resolve the dispute between the Eastern Churches and the Latin Church and to restore unity among Christians;
    b. The council fathers approved the Franciscan and Dominican Orders; and
    c. The council approved the procedures of electing the Supreme Pontiff in a conclave.

11. The Council of Trent (1545-1563).
    a. The council dealt with the challenges of the Protestant Reformation. In so doing, it formulated and introduced the Catholic Catechism to help the lay faithful learn about the Catholic faith;
    b. Responding to the Protestant Reformation, the Church put the accent on moral law, Church authority, and the sacraments. Thus, the Church's missionary activity became more ecclesiastical and less evangelical; and
    c. The council imposed the Roman Liturgy on the Latin Church in an attempt to ensure the uniformity of liturgical celebrations.

12. The First Vatican Council (1869-1870).
    a. The council reaffirmed papal primacy in the governance of the Church; and

    b. The council definitively defined the doctrine of papal infallibility. The Old Catholic Church rejected this doctrine of infallibility, which led to a schism.

13. The Second Vatican Council (1962-1965).
    a. The council fathers issued various pastoral and disciplinary documents; and
    b. The council called for a renewal of the Roman Rite liturgy, discussed the nature of the Church, its relations to the modern world, and promoted Scriptural studies.

Since the Second Vatican Council is the most recent ecumenical council in the Latin Church, it deserves to be explored more extensively.

The Second Vatican Council, from October 11, 1962, through December 8, 1965, was convened by Pope John XXIII. The council was held in four different sessions. The first session, from October 11, 1962 to December 8, 1962, was held under the pontificate of Pope John XXIII. He died on June 3, 1963. Pope Paul VI was elected on June 21, 1963, and he reconvened the Second Vatican Council. The remaining three sessions of the council were held under the leadership of Pope Paul VI.

The second session was held from September 29, 1963 to December 4, 1963, under the leadership of Pope Paul VI. The most important documents the council issued in the second session include *Sacrosanctum Concilium* (The Constitution on the Sacred Liturgy; December 4, 1963) and *Inter Mirifica* (Decree on the Means of Social Communication; December 4, 1963).

The third session was held from September 14 1964 to November 21, 1964. At the end of the third session, the council fathers issued the following documents:

- *Lumen Gentium* (Dogmatic Constitution on the Church; November 21, 1964);
- *Orientalium Ecclesiarum* (Decree on the Catholic Eastern Churches; November 21, 1964); and
- *Unitatis Redintegratio* (Decree on Ecumenism; November 21, 1964).

The fourth session was held from September 14, 1965 to December 8, 1965. The fourth session issued the following documents:

- *Christus Dominus* (Decree on the Pastoral Office of Bishops in the Church; October 28, 1965);
- *Perfectae Caritatis* (Decree on the up-to-date Renewal of Religious Life; October 28, 1965);
- *Optatem Totius* (Decree on the Training of Priests; October 28, 1965);
- *Gravissimum Educationis* (Declaration on Christian Education; October 28, 1965);
- *Nostra Aetate* (Declaration on the Relation of the Church to Non-Christian Religions; October 28, 1965);
- *Dei Verbum* (Dogmatic Constitution on Divine Revelation; November 18, 1965);
- *Apostolicam Actuositatem* (Decree on the Apostolate of Lay people; November 18, 1965);
- *Dignitatis Humanae* (Declaration on Religious Liberty; December 7, 1965);
- *Ad Gentes Divinitus* (Decree on the Church's Missionary Activity; December 7, 1965);
- *Presbyterorum Ordinis* (Decree on the Ministry and Life of Priests; December 7, 1965); and
- *Gaudium et Spes* (Pastoral Constitution on the Church in the Modern World; December 7, 1965).

According to O'Malley (2008), the documents of the Second Vatican Council vary in rank. The documents with the highest rank are the "constitutions," which are:

- The Constitution on the Sacred Liturgy;
- The Dogmatic Constitution on the Church;
- The Dogmatic Constitution on Divine Revelation; and
- The Pastoral Constitution on the Church in the Modern World.

The second highest in rank are the nine decrees the council issued:

- On social communications;

- On the Catholic Eastern Churches;
- On ecumenism;
- On bishops;
- On the renewal of religious life;
- On the training of priests;
- On the ministry and life of priests;
- On the apostolate of the laity; and
- On missionary activity.

The third highest in rank are the three declarations:

- On Christian education;
- On the Church's relations with non-Christians; and
- On religious liberty.

Unlike the previous general councils of the Latin Church, the Second Vatican Council presented a new ecclesiology on the Church in its document *Lumen Gentium* (The Dogmatic Constitution on the Church), where the council speaks of the Church as the people of God. In this document, the council fathers highlight three important relationships in the Church:

- The relationship between the bishops and the Roman Pontiff;
- The relationship between clergy and laity; and
- The relationship between the Church and other Christian Churches and ecclesial communities as well.

The Second Vatican Council presents a new perspective of a Church that is more biblical, inclusive, and pastoral. Thus, the significant contributions of the Second Vatican Council include:

- The use of the vernacular in the liturgy;
- The Church's improved relations with non-Catholic Churches and ecclesial communities;
- The Church's newfound witness to dialogue with the world;
- The Church's dialogue with non-Christian religions; and
- More importantly, the council's call on the Church to reflect on itself.

Thus, the council provided a significant reflection on what it means to be a Church, the Church's duties, and the roles and duties of the individual members of the Church. The Second Vatican Council is significant and important because it helped the Church to see itself and its contribution to the modern world and has given rise to consultative bodies, such as the Synod of Bishops, which collaborates with the Supreme Pontiff in addressing the pressing issues confronting the Church at the regional and universal levels.

What does the term "consistory" mean?

A consistory is an assembly of the College of Cardinals, convened and chaired by the pope, to discuss pressing issues affecting the universal Church. Thus, the cardinals are able to "assist the supreme pastor of the Church through collegial action in consistories in which they are gathered by order of the Roman Pontiff who presides over" (c. 353 § 1).

Consistories may be ordinary or extraordinary (general congregation). An ordinary consistory is an assembly of all of the cardinals, and most especially those who reside in Rome, to discuss serious, but recurring, issues affecting the universal Church. In ordinary consistories, the assembled cardinals may carry out acts, such as the creation of new cardinals, the canonization of saints, and the postulation for the pallium for the newly appointed metropolitan archbishops. Though only cardinals are admitted as members of an ordinary consistory, some ordinary consistories that are of particular solemnity, such as the creation of new cardinals or the canonization of saints, often have a public character and are therefore open to other clerics, to members of the diplomatic corps, and to others as guests (c. 353 § 4).

An ordinary consistory during which new cardinals are created is always a solemn celebration. After a liturgical greeting, the Holy Father reads the formula of creation and solemnly proclaims the names of the new cardinals. Following the liturgy of the Word, the Holy Father gives:

- A homily, during which he highlights the significance of the College of Cardinals;

- The profession of faith;
- The taking of the oath by the new cardinals;
- The giving of the red biretta or hat; and
- The assignment of the titular or diaconate church in Rome as a sign that the new cardinals will participate in the pastoral ministry of the local church in Rome.

In placing the red biretta on the head of each newly created cardinal, who kneels before him, the Holy Father speaks to him individually, saying:

> This red hat is a sign of the dignity of a cardinal, meaning that you must be ready to behave with courage, up to the shedding of blood, for the increase of the Christian faith, for the peace and tranquility of the people of God, and for the freedom and spreading of the Holy Roman Church.

The Holy Father then hands the Bull of Creation to the cardinal and the assignment of a titular or diaconate church, which is followed by the exchange of peace with the new cardinal. The cardinals then exchange peace with each other. The celebration concludes with the Prayer of the Faithful, the Lord's Prayer, and the final papal blessing.

An extraordinary consistory, also known as a plenary consistory, is an assembly of all the members of the College of Cardinals to address urgent challenges of the Church. An extraordinary consistory deals with urgent issues, such as Roman Curia reform, Vatican finances, and other serious issues of a pastoral, organizational, or governmental nature that affect the universal Church. All cardinals, including those who do not reside in Rome, are always invited to attend an extraordinary consistory.

Who governs the universal Church when the Apostolic See is vacant?

The Apostolic See is vacant when the pope dies or resigns. Between the time the pope dies or resigns and the election of a new pope, the governance of the universal Church is entrusted to the College of Cardinals. They attend to the daily ordinary business, the handling of those matters that cannot be postponed, and the preparation for the election of a new pope. However, the College of Cardinals "has no power or jurisdiction in matters which pertain to the Supreme Pontiff during his lifetime or in the exercise of his office. Such matters are to be reserved completely and exclusively to the future pope" (*UDR,* 1). As soon as the dean of the College of Cardinals is informed of the death of the pope, he informs all the cardinals and then summons them to Rome for a congregation of the college. He informs the diplomatic corps accredited to the Holy See and the heads of various countries.

During the vacancy of the Apostolic See, the Cardinal Secretary of State, all the heads of the dicasteries of the Roman Curia, that is, the prefects of the congregations, the presidents of the pontifical councils and their secretaries cease to exercise their offices. However, the Major Penitentiary and his officials continue to exercise their ordinary duties, submitting matters they usually refer to the Supreme Pontiff to the College of Cardinals.

During this time, the College of Cardinals creates two kinds of congregations within the college: general congregation and particular congregation. The general congregation includes the whole college, which meets before the beginning of the election of a new pope. The particular congregation is made up of the Cardinal Camerlengo of the Holy Roman Catholic Church and three cardinals, one from each order of the college, that is, the order of bishops, the order of priests, and the order of deacons. The three cardinals are chosen by lot from among the cardinals already in Rome. The offices of these three cardinals and their assistants are dissolved on the conclusion of the third full day. Three other cardinals who are chosen by the same method replace them.

The general congregation of the College of Cardinals handles the more important matters affecting the Church, while recurring issues of less importance are administered by the particular congregation. The general congregations of the college are held in the Apostolic Palace in Vatican City. At these congregations, the dean of the college presides, and if he is impeded, the sub-dean presides. At the first general gathering, each cardinal is given a copy of the Apostolic Constitution *UDG.* The general congregation decides on the day, hour, and manner in which the body of the deceased pope is to be brought to the Vatican

Basilica for public viewing. The burial is to take place between the fourth and sixth day after the death of the pope.

The election of the Roman Pontiff:

The cardinals have an exclusive right to elect the Roman Pontiff. Under the current law governing the election of the Bishop of Rome, only cardinals who are under the age of eighty on the day the See of Rome becomes vacant can vote in the conclave. In theory, any baptized male Catholic can be elected pope, but the *1983 Code of Canon Law* says the one who is elected must be ordained as a bishop before taking canonical possession of his office as Bishop of Rome. Since the fifteenth century, the electors have always chosen a fellow cardinal. All cardinal electors who have been called to Rome for the election of a new pope are to respond immediately.

The cardinal electors gathered in a conclave to elect the new pope swear an oath to observe the prescriptions as dictated by the Apostolic Constitution, which regulates the election of a new pope. The same oath is to be taken by the cardinals who arrive late and subsequently participate in the conclave. The oath, which is read aloud by the dean of the College of Cardinals, is to follow the format below:

> We, the cardinals of the Holy Roman Catholic Church, of the Order of Bishops, of Priests, and of Deacons, promise, pledge, and swear, as a body and individually, to observe exactly and faithfully all the norms contained in the Apostolic Constitution Universi Dominici gregis of the Supreme Pontiff John Paul II, and to maintain rigorous secrecy with regard to matters in any way related to the election of the Roman Pontiff or those which, by their very nature, during the vacancy of the Apostolic See, call for the same secrecy.

After this oath has been taken, each cardinal adds: "And I, (name) cardinal (name) so promise, pledge, and swear." Placing his hand on the Gospel, each cardinal will add: "So help me God and these Gospels which I now touch with my hands."

The conclave takes place within the territory of the Vatican City, in a determined area and building, closed to unauthorized people. From the beginning of the election until its conclusion and the public announcement of a new pope, the cardinals electors are absolutely forbidden to communicate with outside world either by writing, telephone, e-mail, or text messaging.

Procedure of electing Roman Pontiff:

Each vote begins with the preparation and distribution of ballot papers by two non-cardinals who act as the masters of ceremonies. The names of nine voting cardinals are chosen at random:

- Three to serve as scrutineers, or voting judges;
- Three to collect the vote of any sick cardinals who remain in their quarters at the *Domus Sanctae Marthae;* and
- Three "revisers," who check the vote of the scrutineers.

After the ballot papers have been distributed, the non-cardinals are asked to leave the chapel.

The voting process is carried out in three phases:

1. Pre-Scrutiny Phase. This phase is charged with:

    a. The preparation and distribution of the ballot papers by the masters of ceremonies; and
    b. The drawing by lot from the cardinal electors of three scrutineers and three people charged with collecting the votes of the sick.

2. Scrutiny Phase. This phase comprised of:

    a. Placing the ballot in an appropriate receptacle;
    b. The mixing and counting of the ballots; and
    c. The opening of the votes.

3. Post-Scrutiny Phase. This phase comprised of:

    a. The counting of the votes;

  b. The checking of the same; and
  c. The burning of the ballots.

The ballot paper is rectangular. On the top, the Latin phrase *Eligo in Summum Pontificem* (I elect as the most Supreme Pontiff) is printed and the lower half is blank for the writing of the name of the person chosen. Each voting cardinal then writes out the name of his choice secretly and legibly and then folds the paper twice. The ballot papers from sick cardinals are collected and brought back to the chapel.

Each cardinal then walks to the altar, holding up his folded ballot so it can be seen and says aloud:

> I call as my witness Christ the Lord, who will be my judge that my vote is given to the one who before God I think should be elected.

The cardinal places his ballot on a plate or paten, then slides it into an urn or large chalice. When all the ballots have been cast, the first scrutineer shakes the urn to mix them up. He then transfers the ballots to a new urn, counting them to make sure they correspond to the number of electors. The ballots are read out. Each of the three scrutineers examines each ballot one by one, with the last scrutineer calling out the name on the ballot, so all the cardinals can record the tally. The last scrutineer pierces each ballot with a needle through the word *Eligo* and places it on a thread, so they can be secured. After the names have been read out, the votes are counted to see if anyone has obtained the two-thirds majority needed for election.

The ballot papers are burned with chemical additives to produce white smoke when a pope has been elected; otherwise, the ballot papers are burned with other chemicals to produce black smoke. If a new pope is not elected after twelve or thirteen days into the conclave, the cardinals must move to a run-off between the top two vote-getters.

When a new pope has been elected by a two-thirds majority of the cardinal electors, the cardinal dean, or the most senior cardinal, in the name of the whole college, asks the consent of the one elected by saying, "Do you accept your canonical election as the Supreme Pontiff?" Once the one elected gives consent, he is asked a second question, "By what name do you wish to be called?" Once the elected person accepts his canonical election, he immediately becomes the Bishop of Rome and the head of the College of Bishops if he is already a bishop. Otherwise, he is immediately ordained as a bishop by the cardinal dean, after which he assumes the duties and rights of the office of the Roman Pontiff.

Is there any difference between a Catholic university and an ecclesiastical university?

The Catholic Church has an innate right to establish and operate institutions such as Catholic universities, colleges, and ecclesiastical universities to promote higher learning in any field of knowledge. Such institutions of higher education contribute to the advancement of the people and the fulfillment of the Church's teaching mission. The Church's institutions of higher learning fall under two main categories: Catholic universities/colleges and ecclesiastical universities or faculties.

Catholic universities and ecclesiastical universities or faculties are centers of creativity and the dissemination of knowledge for the good of humanity. These institutions of higher learning are dedicated "to research, to teaching, and to the education of students who freely associate with their teachers in a common love of knowledge. Every university shares the joy of searching for, discovery, and communicating truth in every field of knowledge" (*ECE*, 15). It is in the light of this insight that John Masefield, an English poet and renowned scholar, describes a university as "a place where those who hate ignorance may strive to know; where those who perceive truth may strive to make others see it." Before delving into the differences between a Catholic university and an ecclesiastical university or faculties, the author first discusses the concept of a "Catholic university" and "ecclesiastical university or faculty" as discussed.

Pope John Paul II described a Catholic university as "a place of research, where scholars scrutinize reality with the methods proper to each academic discipline, in order to contribute to the treasury of human knowledge" (*ECE*, 15). Research in a Catholic university should focus on the search for an integration of knowledge, a dialogue between faith and reason, an ethical concern, and a theological perspective (*ECE,* 15). The distinctive characteristics of a Catholic university, according to Pope John Paul II, are:

a. A Christian inspiration, not only of individual members, but of the university community as such;
b. A continuing reflection in the light of the Catholic faith upon the growing treasury of human knowledge, to which it seeks to contribute to its own research;
c. Fidelity to the Christian message as it comes to us through the Church; and
d. An institutional commitment to the service of the people of God and of the human family in their pilgrimage to the transcendent goal that gives meaning to life.

It is evident from the aforementioned characteristics that, in addition to research and services common to all universities, a Catholic university has its own mission, which includes the following:

- Service to the Church and society;
- Pastoral ministry to its students;
- Cultural dialogue; and
- Evangelization.

As a Catholic institution of higher learning, a Catholic university must perform its research projects, teaching, and all other activities with Catholic ideals, principles, and attitudes in a manner that it is linked with "the Church either by a formal, constitutive, and statutory bond or by reason of an institutional commitment made by those responsible for its existence" (*ECE*, 2, § 2).

A Catholic university may be established by the Holy See, by episcopal conference, by another assembly of the Catholic hierarchy, or by a diocesan bishop. A Catholic university may also be established by a religious order or a society of apostolic life or other public juridical person. A Catholic layperson or persons may also establish a Catholic university, but such a university can be called a "Catholic university" only with the consent of a competent ecclesiastical authority, because "no university is to bear the title or name of

Catholic university without the consent of competent ecclesiastical authority" (c. 808).

An ecclesiastical university or faculty is also a center for higher learning with a special focus on theological disciplines, such as Scripture; fundamental, dogmatic, and pastoral theology; liturgy; Church history; canon law; philosophy; archeology; and other social sciences that are related to these sacred disciplines. Ecclesiastical universities or faculties are established to investigate the sacred disciplines and to instruct students scientifically in the same disciplines that "are proper to the Church by virtue of its function to announce the revealed truth" (c. 815).

Canon 816 asserts that ecclesiastical universities or faculties can only "be established through erection by the Apostolic See or with its approval; their higher direction also pertains to it." Though there are many Catholic universities and colleges in the United States, only few have ecclesiastical faculties. For instance, the Catholic University of America in Washington, DC, has three ecclesiastical faculties: the departments of theology, canon law, and the school of philosophy. Most of the pontifical universities in Rome are ecclesiastical universities.

The difference between a Catholic university and an ecclesiastical university is seen in the areas of:

1. Establishment:

    a. While any competent ecclesiastical authority in the Church, such as the bishops' conference, bishops in a given ecclesiastical province, a diocesan bishop, or a juridical person can establish a Catholic university, the Apostolic See has the exclusive right to the establishment of an ecclesiastical university or its approval.
    b. A physical person or persons may establish a Catholic university with the consent of a competent ecclesiastical authority.

2. Apostolic Constitution:

    a. While the Apostolic Constitution, *Ex corde Ecclesiae,* regulates the internal organization of Catholic universities and colleges; the Apostolic Constitution, *Sapientia christiana,* regulates the operation and organization of ecclesiastical universities and faculties.

3. Areas of study:

    a. Unlike a Catholic university which can have different disciplines of study including medicine, law, business courses, physical sciences, and many other areas of study in addition to theological disciplines, an ecclesiastical university focuses on the sacred disciplines such as Scripture, theology, canon law, philosophy, and other related social science courses. The Church confides the task of preparing its students for the priesthood and for teaching and holding ecclesiastical positions to ecclesiastical universities and faculties.

    b. Individual ecclesiastical universities or faculties are to have their own statutes of governance as well as programs of studies. These statutes and plans of studies must be drawn up in accordance with the requirements of *Sapientia christiana* and must be approved by the Apostolic See. Catholic universities have their own statutes of governance and programs of studies, but they do not need any approval from the Apostolic See when formulating their statutes and plans of academic studies. However, Catholic theologians who teach theological disciplines in Catholic colleges and universities must be "faithful to the magisterium of the Church as the authentic interpreter of sacred Scripture and sacred tradition" (*ECE* article 4 § 3). The non-Catholic professors and students in Catholic colleges and universities must recognize and respect the distinctive Catholic identity of their institutions.

4. Degrees:

    a. Only ecclesiastical universities or faculties can award or confer academic degrees that have canonical effects on the Church. Catholic universities that do not have ecclesiastical faculties cannot confer academic degrees, such as the licentiate in theology, Scripture, or canon law that have canonical effects. Catholic universities can only confer civil academic degrees. Similarly, ecclesiastical universities that do not have a civil charter cannot award or confer civil academic degrees. Since academic degrees such as the master's degree (MA) or the doctor of philosophy degree (PhD) are civil degrees, they can only be conferred by civil universities or Catholic universities that have a civil charter.

From the above, there is a clear distinction between Catholic universities and the ecclesiastical universities or faculties. Though distinct, Catholic universities and ecclesiastical universities or faculties participate in the evangelizing mission of the Church. The education of students, whether in a Catholic university or in an ecclesiastical university, "is to combine academic and professional development with the formation in moral and religious principles and the social teachings of the Church. The program of studies for each of the various professions is to include an appropriate ethical formation in that profession" (*ECE,* 5).

Ecclesiastical universities or faculties award the following academic titles:

- BTh,   Bachelor of Theology;
- DD,   Doctor of Divinity;
- DTh,   Doctor of Theology;
- JCD,   Doctor of Canon Law;
- JCL,   Licentiate in Canon Law;
- JUD,   Juris Utriuqe Doctoris (Doctor of both canon laws in the Latin Church and Eastern Catholic Churches);
- LTh,   Licentiate in Theology;
- MD,   Master of Divinity;
- MTh,   Master of Sacred Theology;
- SSD,   Doctor of Sacred Scripture;
- SSL,   Licentiate in Sacred Scripture;
- SSM,   Master in Sacred Sciences;
- STD,   Doctor of Sacred Theology;
- STL,   Licentiate in Sacred Theology; and

- STM,   Master in Sacred Theology.

As noted above, ecclesiastical degrees in these sacred sciences that the Church awards have canonical importance. The Church often recommends those individuals who are undergoing formation for leadership roles in the Church be trained in these academic disciplines.

Does the Roman Catholic Church have any relationship with other Christian Churches and ecclesial communities?

The Catholic Church has a close relationship with other Christian Churches and ecclesial communities. The Second Vatican Council defines, informs, and directs the Church's relations with other Churches and ecclesial communities when it asserts that all those who have been justified by faith in baptism are incorporated in Christ's Church and, therefore, have a right to be called Christians (*UR*, 3).

The Eastern Christian Churches, also known as "the Orthodox Churches," although separated from the Catholic Church, possess true sacraments, most especially the priesthood and the Eucharist, by virtue of unbroken apostolic succession and, therefore, enjoy the closest intimacy with the Catholic Church. The other Christian Churches and ecclesial communities "are bound to the Catholic Church by a specially close relationship as a result of the long span of earlier centuries when the Christian people had lived in ecclesial communion" (*UR*, 19).

The Catholic Church has different levels of relationships with other Christian churches and ecclesial communities. Below are the different levels of the relationships:

1. Reception of Baptism and Confirmation:

    a. The Catholic Church teaches that one is incorporated into Christ and his Church by baptism. The Catholic Church recognizes baptism conferred with a proper form and matter in some other Churches and ecclesial communities as valid.
    b. The Catholic Church views the role that godparents or Christian witnesses play in the life of the person they

sponsored in a liturgical and canonical sense. Liturgically and canonically, the godparents should be members of the Church or ecclesial community in which the sacrament is celebrated. The duty of the godparents is not only to facilitate the formation of the person being baptized in the practice of the faith, but also to act as representatives of a community of faith, guaranteeing the candidate's faith and desire for ecclesial communion. But because of the "close relationship between the Catholic Church and the Eastern Orthodox Churches, the Catholic Church can allow an Eastern non-Catholic to act as godparent at the baptism of a Catholic infant" (*DE,* 98b). A baptized person who belongs to an ecclesial community is also allowed to act as a witness at a baptism in a Catholic Church.

2. Common Prayer with Christians of Other Churches and Ecclesial Communities:

   a. One also sees the Church's relationship with other Churches and ecclesial communities when it encourages Catholic Christians to join in prayer service with Christians of other Churches and ecclesial communities. Such common prayer services can promote peace among Catholics and other Christians (*DE,* 108).

3. Sharing of Church Building:

   a. Though Catholic church buildings are consecrated and reserved for Catholic worship only, the local ordinary may allow other Churches or ecclesial communities to use Catholic church buildings for their liturgical services, if they do not have a place of their own (*DE,* 137). Similarly, the local ordinary may, for a just cause and provided scandals are avoided, permit a Catholic priest to celebrate the Eucharist in the place of worship of another Church or ecclesial community (c. 933).

4. Liturgies of Marriages:

a. A Marriage in Eastern Churches:

    i. Because of its relationship with other Christian Churches and ecclesial communities, the Catholic Church allows a Catholic priest or deacon to participate in the celebration of a marriage that is "properly celebrated between Eastern Christians or between a Catholic and an Eastern Christian in the Eastern Church, if invited to do so by the Eastern Church authority" (*DE*, 127).

b. A Marriage in non-Eastern Churches and Ecclesial Communities:

    i. The *1998 Directory for the application of principles and norms on Ecumenism* allows members of non-Eastern Churches and ecclesial communities to act as witnesses at the celebration of a marriage in a Catholic church. Similarly, Catholic faithful may be admitted as witnesses at a marriage that is celebrated in non-Eastern churches or ecclesial communities (*DE*, 136).

    ii. A Catholic priest or deacon may participate in some way in the celebration of a mixed marriage, provided dispensation from canonical form has been granted. At such celebrations, "the Catholic priest or deacon may offer some appropriate prayers, read from the Scriptures, give a brief exhortation, and bless the couple" (*DE*, 157).

    iii. Similarly upon the request of the couple, "the local ordinary may permit the Catholic priest to invite the minister of the party of the non-Eastern Church or ecclesial community to participate in the celebration of the marriage, to read from the Scriptures, give a belief exhortation, and bless the couple" (*DE*, 158).

5. Sharing of the Sacramentals:

    a. Blessing:

        i. A Catholic priest may administer a blessing on non-Catholic Christians when they voluntarily ask for a Catholic blessing.

    b. Funeral Services and Christian Burial:

        i. The diocesan bishop may, under certain circumstances, allow non-Catholic Christian ministers to celebrate funeral services in a Catholic church, if the non-Catholic Christians do not have their own place of worship.
        ii. The diocesan bishop may also allow non-Catholic Christians to be buried in a Catholic cemetery (*DE*, 137).

From the aforementioned discussion, one can conclude that the Catholic Church has created a friendly environment to promote an active relationship with members of other Christian Churches and ecclesial communities. The Catholic Church is committed to promoting a healthy relationship with other Christian Churches and ecclesial communities and has charged the pontifical council for promotion of Christian unity with the task of cultivating relationships with other Churches and ecclesial communities. The Catholic Church's relationships with other Churches and ecclesial communities should be based on mutual respect for the individual traditions, disciplines, and autonomy of each Christian denomination.

REFERENCES

Arrieta, J. I. (2000). *Governance structures within the Catholic Church.* Montreal, Canada: Wilson & Lafleur Ltée.

Bachofen, A. (1926). *The canonical and civil status of Catholic parishes in the United States.* St. Louis, MO: Herder Books Co.

Beal, J. P. (2000). Marriage. In John P. Beal, James A. Coriden, & James J. Green (Eds.), *New commentary on the code of canon law* (pp. 1234-1392). New York: Paulist Press.

Beal, J. P., Coriden, J. A., & Green, T. J. (2000). *New commentary on the code of canon law.* New York: Paulist Press.

Cardinal Kasper, W. (2003). *Leadership in the Church: How traditional roles can serve the Christian community today.* New York: A Herder & Herder Book.

Congregation for Catholic Education. (1988). *The religious dimension of education in Catholic school: Guidelines for reflection and renewal.* Rome: The Author.

Congregation for Divine Worship (1988). *Directory for Sunday celebration in the absence of presbyter.* Rome: The Author.

Coriden, J. A. (1997). *The parish in Catholic tradition: History, theology, and canon law.* New York: Paulist Press.

Donovan, D. (1997). *Distinctively Catholic: An exploration of Catholic identity.* New York: Paulist Press.

Doohan (1984). *The lay-centered church: Theology and spirituality.* New York: Harper & Row.

Dulles, A. (1984). The teaching authority of bishops' conference. in *America, 148*, 453-455.

Dulles, A. (1988a). The mandate to teach. *America, 162*, 293-295.

Dulles, A. (1988b). What is the role of a bishops' conference. *Origins, 17*, 790-796.

Feliciani, I. (1988). Episcopal conferences from Vatican II to the 1983 code. *The Jurist 48*, 11-25.

Flannery, A. (Ed.). (1998). *Vatican II: The conciliar and post-conciliar documents.* Northport, NY: Costello Publishing Co.

Granfield, P. (1987). *The limits of the papacy: Authority and autonomy in the Church.* New York: Crossroad.

Green, T. J. (1987). *Conferences of bishops and the exercise of the "munus docendi of the church.* Rome: Gregorian University.

Huels, J. M. (2000). Other acts of divine worship (cc. 116-1204). In J. P. Beal, J. A. Coriden, & T. J. Green (Eds.). *New commentary on the code of canon law* (pp. 1400-1423). Mahwah, NJ: Paulist Press.

Huels, J. M. (2001). Lecture notes, St. Paul University, Ottawa, Canada.

Huels, J. M. (2009). *The pastoral companion: A canon law handbook for Catholic ministry.* Montreal, Canada: Wilson & Lafleur Ltée.

Kikoti, W. P. (1996). *Episcopal conferences in the light of Vatican II: Theological foundation and role in the Church. A case study of Tanzanian episcopal conference.* Rome: Pontificia Universitas Urbanian.

Kutner, R. (1972). *The development, structure and competence of episcopal conference.* Washington, DC: Catholic University of America Press.

Libreria Editrice Vaticana. (1994). *Catechism of the Catholic Church.* Liguori, MO: Liguori Publications.

Martin De Agar, J. T. (1999). *A handbook on canon law.* Montreal, Canada: Wilson & Lafeur Ltée.

O'Malley, J. W. (2008). *What happened at Vatican II.* Cambridge, MA: Harvard University Press.

Paul V (1968). Apostolic constitution: *Pontificalis Romani recognition.* Rome, The Author.

Pope Benedict XV1. (2008). Address to Catholic educators at the Catholic University of America. In *Christ our hope: Pope Benedict XVI's Apostolic journey to the United States and visit to the United Nations.* 42-45.

Pope John Paul II (1983). *Divinus prefectionis magister (Apostolic constitution).* Vatican: Libreria Edictrice Vaticana.

Ratziner, J. (1984). Among priests and bishops in J. Ratzinger and V. Messor, *Ratziner's report,* San Francisco: Ignatius Press; 55-69.

Reese, T. (1996). *Inside the Vatican: The politics and organization of the Catholic Church.* Cambridge, MA: Harvard University Press.

Sacred Congregation for Clergy. (1971). *General catechetical directory.* Rome: The Author.

Urrutia, F. J. (1989). De exercitio muneris docendi a conferentiis episcoporum, *Periodica, 76.* 602-622,

Woestman, W. H. (2000). *Ecclesiastical sanctions and the penal process. A commentary on the code of canon law.* Ottawa, Canada: St. Paul University Press.

GLOSSARY

Ad limina. A formal visit that diocesan bishops and those who are equivalent to them in law must make to Rome to the "thresholds of the Apostles Peter and Paul" and to present themselves before the Roman Pontiff to give an account of the state of their dioceses. During *Ad limina* visits, diocesan bishops of a given country or region make a pilgrimage to the tombs of the apostles and then show the proper reverence for the pope, the Successor of Peter, thereby acknowledging his universal jurisdiction over the Church by giving an account of the state of the particular churches in their country or region and receiving his admonition and counsel. Such visits bind relations between the Roman Pontiff and his brother bishops more closely.

Apostolic administrator. A priest or a bishop who has been named by the Apostolic See to govern a diocese when the diocesan see is impeded or becomes vacant.

Apostolic camera. A central board of finance in the Roman Curia that supervises the governance of the states of the Church and the administration of justice. This board is led by the Camerlengo of the Holy Roman Church.

Apostolic constitution. A formal document issued by the Supreme Pontiff on matters of doctrinal or juridical importance for the universal Church.

Canon law. A body of laws, divine and ecclesiastical, and universal and particular of the Roman Catholic Church. The term also refers to all laws governing the Eastern Catholic Churches.

Canonical form. A formal requirement of the Catholic Church that a marriage in which both parties are Catholics or even when one of the parties is Catholic must be celebrated before two witnesses and a priest or a deacon who has the lawful faculty to assist at marriage (c. 1108).

Censure. A penalty that may be imposed on an errant member of the Catholic faithful. Censure may be an excommunication, an interdict, or a suspension (cc. 1331-1338).

Christian faithful *(Christifidelis)*. The term refers to all baptized people, a community of believers in Christ Jesus (c. 204). Canonically, the term "Christian faithful" as used in c. 204 refers to all baptized people, Catholics and non-Catholic Christians, whose baptism is recognized by the Catholic Church.

Church building. A building designated for divine worship to which the Catholic faithful have a right of entry for the celebration of the liturgy and other sacraments (c. 1214).

Church *sui iuris*. A community of Catholic faithful united by its own hierarchy, liturgical tradition, and discipline, but which recognizes the pope's authority and is in full communion with him (the pope). Some examples of Church *sui iuris* are the Latin Church, Maronite Catholic Church, Ukrainian Catholic Church, and Coptic Catholic (c. 1).

Cleric. An ordained member of the Catholic faithful: a deacon, presbyter, or bishop.

College of Bishops. All bishops all over the world who are in communion with the pope (c. 36).

College of consultors. A group of priests (may include auxiliary and coadjutor bishops) selected from among the diocesan priests' council to assist and advise the diocesan bishop on certain pertinent matters pertaining to the pastoral governance of his diocese. The group consists of six to twelve members (c. 502).

Concordat. A formal agreement or treaty signed between the Vatican and a secular government relating to matters of mutual interest.

Consecrated life. Catholic faithful who have been consecrated by the profession of evangelical counsels. People in consecrated life include hermits, virgins, and people in religious institutes and secular institutes or other forms recognized by the Apostolic See (cc. 573, 605).

Consent (matrimonial). A free choice made between a man and a woman to marry each other (c. 1057).

Consummation (matrimonial). The first sexual intercourse, freely consented to and open to procreation, between a husband and his wife after they have given and accepted each other in a valid marriage. To constitute a human act, the sexual intercourse must be performed willingly and mutually (c. 1061).

Convalidation. A legal remedy by which a previously invalid marriage is made valid (c. 1156). This remedy may be a simple convalidation (c. 1156) or may be done through a canonical process called *sanatio in radice* (retroactive validation) (c. 1160).

Curia. Some appointed or selected persons who assist an ecclesiastical authority, such as the pope, Eastern patriarchs, or diocesan bishop in the pastoral governance of the Church. It may be the Roman Curia, in which case the selected curial officials assist the Supreme Pontiff in the pastoral governance of the universal Church, or a diocesan curia, where the curial officials assist the diocesan bishop in the governance of his local church. The selected persons who assist in curial capacity often exercise pastoral, administrative, and judicial functions (c. 469).

Danger of death. In law, any condition of being at risk of dying because of illness, injury, execution, or any other life-threatening causes (c. 1079).

Dicastery. A generic term used for any of the departments of the Roman Curia. Thus, the term refers to the congregations, tribunals, pontifical councils, and other offices of the Roman Curia.

Dimissorial letter. A formal letter written by one's ordinary to the ordaining bishop testifying that the candidate being admitted into the Holy Orders has met all necessary requirements for ordination (cc. 1050-1052).

Disparity of cult. An impediment that prevents a valid marriage between a Catholic and non-baptized person (c. 1086).

Dispensation. The act of giving a concession from an ecclesiastical law or discipline for the spiritual benefit of a person in a particular case. Dispensation can only be given by an ecclesiastical person who is capable (c. 85).

Divine office. Also known as the liturgy of the holy hours, this is an ancient form of a Christian prayer that is to be celebrated at different times or hours of the day and night.

Eastern Christian Churches. Orthodox Christian Churches such as the Coptic Orthodox, Maronite Orthodox, Greek Orthodox, and Russian Orthodox Churches.

Ecclesial community. A Christian denomination that the Roman Catholic Church does not recognize as having all the essential elements to constitute it as a Church. The term generally refers to Protestant denominations (c. 844).

Ecclesiastical law. The man-made law in the Roman Catholic Church, as opposed to a divine law (c. 11).

Ecclesiastical province. A territorial unit consisting of all particular churches in a given area. An ecclesiastical province is headed by an archbishop who is a metropolitan archbishop. The diocesan bishops under a metropolitan archbishop in a given ecclesiastical province are known as suffragan bishops.

Ecumenical council. A solemn assembly of the College of Bishops and the pope that exercises supreme power and determines or defines important doctrinal and disciplinary matters for the universal Church (cc. 337-341).

Excardination. A canonical process by which a cleric relinquishes his canonical attachment to a diocese, an institute of consecrated life, or a society of apostolic life in order to be incardinated in another diocese, institute of consecrated life, or society of apostolic life (cc. 270-272).

Expiatory penalty. A type of penalty that may be imposed on errant members of the Church perpetually, temporally, or indefinitely (c. 1336).

Extraordinary minister. A person who performs a liturgical function when the number of ordinary ministers is insufficient for pastoral needs. For instance, a layperson may distribute Holy Communion during Sunday liturgy in a Catholic Church (c. 230 § 3).

Faculty. A power or authorization given by law or delegation enabling the recipient of the faculty to validly perform an act in the name of the Church.

Incardination. A canonical process by which a cleric is juridically attached to a diocese, an institute of consecrated life, or a society of apostolic life. One is incardinated to a diocese of an institute of consecrated life or a society of apostolic life by virtue of one's diaconate ordination (cc. 265-269).

Indulgence. The remission before God of the temporal punishment due for sins whose guilt is already forgiven, which a member of the Christian faithful gains under certain and defined conditions by the assistance of the Church. The conditions under which one gains indulgences are specified in canon 992. An indulgence may be partial or plenary, depending on whether it partially or totally frees one from the temporal punishment due to sins (c. 993).

Infant. In canon law, a person under the age of seven or one who habitually lacks the use of reason (cc. 97 § 2; 99).

Juridic person. An aggregate of persons or things, which may be public or private, established by law or by a competent ecclesiastical authority and ordered for a purpose that is in keeping with the mission of the Church and that transcends the purpose of individuals. Examples of juridical persons in the Church are a diocese, a parish church, a province of a religious institute, a Catholic hospital, a Catholic university, or a charitable foundation (cc. 113-123).

Laicization. The loss of a clerical state by means of a rescript from the Holy See (c. 290).

Latae sententiae penalty. A censure of excommunication, interdict, or suspension that is incurred automatically on an errant member of the Church upon the commission of a canonical crime without going through any canonical process (c. 1314).

Legate (papal legate). A representative of the pope to a nation that has diplomatic relations with the Vatican City. When a papal legate is appointed to represent the pope to a nation and the conference of bishops in a given country, he is called a nuncio. When he represents the pope at the conference of bishops without any diplomatic duties, he is referred to as an apostolic delegate (cc. 362-7).

Liciety. The lawfulness or licitness of a juridical act. Generally in law, liciety does not affect the validity of an act.

Minor. In canon law, a person under eighteen years of age.

Mixed marriage. A marriage between a Catholic and a baptized non-Catholic Christian (c. 1124). In a broad sense, it may include a marriage between a Catholic and non-baptized person.

Non-consummated marriage. A valid marriage in which the parties have not freely and mutually engaged in sexual intercourse, open to procreation, after they have lawfully exchanged matrimonial consent (cc. 1066 § 1 2; 1697-1706).

Non-Eastern Christian Churches. Christian Churches separated from the Apostolic See during the grave crisis that began in the West at the end of the Middle Ages or during later times. The non-Eastern Christian Churches include the Polish National Church, the Old Catholic Church, the Old Roman Catholic Church, and the Society of St. Pius X (SSPX) which was founded by Archbishop Marcel Lefebvre. The SSPX rejects some of the teachings of the Second Vatican Council.

Parochial vicar. A priest who has been appointed to assist the pastor in the pastoral ministry of a parish. A parochial vicar may also be called an associate pastor or a curate (c. 545).

Papal chapel. A group of dignitaries that assists the pope in carrying out religious ceremonies as spiritual leader of the Church.

Papal household. Consists of dignitaries who assist the Roman Pontiff in carrying out certain important ceremonies of either religious or civil character. The papal household is divided into two sections: papal chapel and papal family.

Papal family. Consists of dignitaries who assist the pope in exercising his civil functions as the head of a juridical body.

Particular church. A canonical term for the territorial units of the Latin Church, such as dioceses, territorial prelatures, territorial abbacies, apostolic vicariates, apostolic prefectures, and apostolic administrations erected on a stable basis (c. 368).

Prefecture for the Economic Affairs. An office within the Roman Curia that supervises and governs the administration of the temporal goods that are dependent on the Holy See.

Presbyteral council. A group of priests selected to represent all the priests in a given diocese to assist the diocesan bishop in the pastoral governance of his diocese (c. 495).

Religious institute. Generically, term for a religious order, congregation, or society. Members of a religious institute take public vows of poverty, chastity, and obedience and live in community as brothers or sisters (c. 607).

Sacramentals. Sacred signs which, by the approval of the Church, are celebrated for the spiritual benefits of the Christian faithful through the intercession of the Church (cc. 1166-1172).

Secular institute. An institute of consecrated life whose members' proper canonical state as clerics or laypersons does not change by their consecration.

Shrine. A church or other sacred place to which the Catholic faithful, with the approval of a competent ecclesiastical authority, make pilgrimages for devotional purposes (c. 1230).

Society of apostolic life. A group of Catholic faithful who have organized themselves to undertake an apostolic mission. These Catholic faithful, like the religious, live in common life as brothers or sisters but do not take religious vows (c. 731).

Supreme authority. In canon law, the pope and the College of Bishops acting in communion with the pope.

Synod of Bishops. An assembly of bishops, convoked by the pope, to advise him on pertinent issues affecting the universal Church. A synod of bishops may be general, in which the assembled bishops discuss, study, and advise the pope on matters affecting the entire Church, or may be regional, where the assembled bishops discuss issues affecting the Church in a particular region and give their counsel on those issues to the pope.

Terna. A list of candidates suitable for the office of bishop that the bishops of a given ecclesiastical province are to compose in common counsel and in secret every three years. This list is sent to the papal legate, who in turn forward the list of suitable candidates to the

Apostolic See. It is from this list of candidates that one is chosen and appointed as a bishop whenever the need arises.

Tribunal. A Church court that principally processes cases of marital nullity (cc. 1417-1445).

Validity. The validity of an act refers to the legal efficacy of a juridical act.

INDEX

religious institutes, 40–42, 55, 78,
81, 84, 105, 112, 130, 138, 181,
184, 186
religious order, 33, 41, 46, 149,
166, 186
religious profession, 41, 141
removal from office, 78, 80, 82, 96
rite, 27, 95, 111–12, 119, 138, 141, 156
ritual of circumcision, 31
Roman Curia, 20, 45, 49–51, 53,
61–63, 71, 91, 160–61, 181, 185
Roman Pontiff, 20, 26–27, 43,
47–49, 51–52, 54, 63–66, 71, 73,
75, 78, 85–87, 103–4, 126, 131,
158–59, 162–63, 165, 185
Roman Rota, 50–52, 134

S

sacrament
of anointing of the sick, 96–97,
107, 116–19, 124
of baptism, 29, 31–32, 108, 110
of confession/penance, 116–19,
122–24
of confirmation, 96–97, 107,
110–11
of holy orders, 35, 38, 107, 112
of marriage, 107, 125
non-repeatable, 107
repeatable, 107
sacramentals, 13, 20, 139, 141–42,
173, 186
sacramental sharing, 173
sacred images, 20, 141, 145, 148
sacred place, 149, 186
sanatio in radice (retroactive
validation), 133, 181

Sapientia christiana, 168
schismatics, 145
scrutineer, 164
Second Council of Lyon, 120, 155
Second Council of Nicaea, 152, 154
Second Vatican Council, 28, 34–35,
38, 40, 50, 86, 89–90, 92, 141,
156–59, 170, 185
Secretariat of State, 49–50, 52, 63
Secular institute, 186
secular institutes, 40–42, 181
seminary, 14, 19, 48, 56, 67, 84, 88,
138, 148
shrine, 20, 57, 68, 148–49, 186
Sixtus V (pope), 49
Society of apostolic life, 34, 166,
183, 186
sponsor, 32, 108–9
suffragan bishop, 86–88, 182
Supreme Pontiff, 22, 49, 52–53, 63,
66, 68–71, 74–75, 147, 153, 155,
159, 161, 164, 181
Supreme Tribunal of the Apostolic
Signatura, 51–52, 134–35, 138
Synod of Bishops, 65–68, 159, 186
extraordinary, 66–67
ordinary, 65–67
special, 66, 68

T

teaching office of the church, 39,
102–4, 106
terna, 75, 186
threefold munera, 76, 92
titular bishop, 145
transitional deacon, 112, 144
transubstantiation, 119–21, 155

CPSIA information can be obtained at www.ICGtesting.com
Printed in the USA
BVOW05s1225090914

365977BV00002B/108/P